THE GODLY MAN'S ARK

or,

City of Refuge in the Day of His Distress:
Five Sermons Designed for the Support and Consolation of the
Saints of God in the Time of Affliction.

by Edmund Calamy, B.D., (1600-1666)

COPYRIGHT INFORMATION

CONTENTS

MEET EDMUND CALAMY

[Taken from *Select Memoirs of the English and Scottish Divines*, by Thomas Smith, Published by Puritan Publications, 2012]

MR. CALAMY was born in London in 1600, and educated at Pembrokehall, in the University of Cambridge, where he took his degree of arts in 1619, and that of divinity in 1632. By an early discovery of his opposition to Arminianism, his fellowship was prevented, even when he was justly entitled, both by his standing, his learning, and his unblameable conversation.

The prelatical rulers in the Church of England were strongly inclined to the doctrines of Arminius at this time, and nothing could stand more in the way of preferment, to a person of Mr. Calamy's sentiments, than his publicly asserting and defending them; so that, considering his warm attachment to the Calvinistic doctrines, and his hostilities to those of the Arminian party, now basking in the beams of royal favor, Mr. Calamy had but little to expect. At last, however, he was elected *tanquam socius*, a title peculiar to Pembrokehall; which, though attended with less emolument, was at least as honorable as that of fellow. Sometime after this Mr. Calamy's studious and religious character recommended him to Dr. Felton, the pious and learned bishop of Ely, who made him his domestic chaplain; and while residing in the family, paid him singular marks of affectionate regard, and at last presented him to the vicarage of Mary's in Swaffhamprior, in his own neighborhood, where he became singularly useful to his flock. Still, however, he continued in the family until the bishop's death, when he was chosen one of the lecturers of Edmund's Bury, in the county of Suffolk, where

Jeremiah Burroughs was his fellow laborer. In this place he continued about ten years. Some writers have said, that during his residence in this place he was a strict conformist; but his own declaration, and that of others, affirm the contrary. It is a certain fact, that Mr. Calamy, with about thirty other worthy ministers, were driven out of bishop Wren's diocese, for not conforming to the Visitation Articles and the unhallowed *Book of Sports*. With these abominations he could not comply; and being in favor with the earl of Essex, he preferred him to the living of Richford, a market town in the Marches of Essex, a rectory of considerable value; but it proved ruinous to his health, and brought on a dizziness of the head, that never wholly forsook him.

Upon the death of Dr. Stoughton he was chosen minister of Mary Aldermanbury, London, in 1639. Here he soon acquired a very distinguished reputation, and made a conspicuous appearance, by the active part he took in the important controversy respecting church government, then greatly agitated.

In 1640, he was employed, with several other puritan divines, in composing that famous book, entitled, *Smectymnuus*; which is said to have given the first fatal blow to episcopacy in England. This strange title is made out of the first letters of the names of its various authors, *viz.* Stephen Marshall, Edmund Calamy, Thomas Young, Matthew Newcomen, and William Spurstowe. This treatise is allowed, on all hands, to have been well written. It was done in answer to a book, entitled, *An Humble Remonstrance*, written by the bishop of Exeter. This learned prelate attempted a confutation of *Smectymnuus*; to which the Presbyterians replied. After this, the far-famed Usher, bishop of Armagh, attacked it; but was repulsed by John Milton, the celebrated author of *Paradise Lost*. The activity, the profound knowledge, integrity, and intrepidity; evinced by Mr. Calamy, had raised his reputation, particularly among the Presbyterians, to the first rank of literary fame. He was appointed, by the House of Lords, a member of the subcommittee for accommodating ecclesiastical affairs; and shortly after this he was appointed a member of the assembly of divines. He was an active and zealous man in all their proceedings, and much distinguished, both for his learning and moderation, in the assembly.

Mr. Calamy was one of the most popular preachers in London, and frequently appointed to preach before the long parliament; for which the prelatical party had treated him with unmerited abuse. He was the first, however, who, before the committee of parliament, defended the proposition, that a bishop and presbyter, according to the scriptures, are one office under different appellations. His interest and influence in the city of London was very extensive, and he preached to a numerous and highly respectable audience, composed of the most eminent citizens, and many persons of quality. He was one of the London ministers who declared against the proceedings of the army, and the violent measures that brought on the king's death; an event which he strongly deprecated.

In Cromwell's time Calamy lived as quietly as possible; but sometimes opposed the protector's measures. It is said of Cromwell, that having a wish to put the crown on his own head, he sent for some of the principal divines of the city, as if he made it a matter of conscience, and that he wanted their advice. Mr. Calamy was one of the party, and boldly opposed the project of Cromwell's single government, offering to prove that the thing was not only unlawful, but that it was also impracticable. To the first of these Cromwell readily replied, "That the safety of the people was the supreme law; but, pray, Mr. Calamy, said he, how is it impracticable?" "Because (says Mr. Calamy) the nation will be against you, nine out of ten at least." "But (says Cromwell) what if I wrest the sword from the nine, and put it in the hands of the tenth—Will not that do the business?" In 1659, Mr. Calamy concurred with the Earl of Mansfield, and other great men, in persuading general Monk to bring in the king, that an end might be put to the public confusions. He preached before the parliament the day before they voted the king's restoration to the throne, and was one of these divines that were sent over to Holland on that business; but he had, soon after, cause to regret the hand he had in that unhappy transaction, particularly that he was received without a previous treaty.

On the restoration of Charles, Mr. Calamy was encouraged to hope that considerable favor and indulgence, both to himself and his brethren would still be granted. In June, the same year, he was sworn chaplain in ordinary to his majesty, with several other Presbyterian ministers; but none of them preached more than once before the king in that capacity. About this time Mr. Calamy was often with his majesty at Earl Mansfield, the chamberlain's lodgings, and other places, and had the royal countenance on all occasions. He had a principal hand in drawing up the proposals, at that time presented to the king, respecting church government; which led the way to the Savoy conference. He was also concerned in the concessions made by the declaration of October 25th, the same year; and being one of the commissioners, he was employed, with others, in drawing up the exceptions against the liturgy, as also the reply to the reasons of the Episcopal divines against these exceptions of the Presbyterians. In 1661 he was one of those chosen by the London ministers to represent then in the convocation; but was not permitted to sit in that assembly. He attended the several meetings at the Savoy, where he did everything in his power to effect an accommodation; but without the least effect.

Mr. Calamy preached his farewell sermon on the 17th of August 1662, a week before the act of uniformity took effect. Having consulted with his great friends at court, the following petition was drawn up, and presented to the king, signed by a considerable number of the London ministers:

"May it please your excellent majesty.—Upon former experience of your majesty's tenderness and indulgence to your obedient and loyal subjects, in which number we can clearly reckon ourselves, we, some of the ministers within your city of London, who, by the late act of uniformity, are likely: to be cast out of all public service in the ministry, because we cannot, in conscience, conform in all things required in said *Act*, have taken the boldness humbly to cast ourselves and our concernments at your majesty's feet, desiring that, of your princely wisdom and compassion, you would take some effectual course, whereby we may be continued in the exercise of our ministry, to teach your people their duty to God and your majesty; and we doubt not, but by our dutiful and peaceable carriage therein, we shall render ourselves not altogether unworthy of so great a favor." This petition was presented by Mr. Calamy, Dr. Manton, Dr. Bates, and others, on the third day after the act became in force. Mr. Calamy made a speech on the occasion, stating, that those of his persuasion were ready to contest the point of fidelity to his majesty with any description of men in England: That they little expected to be dealt with in the manner they had been; and that they were now come before his majesty, imploring his interference in their behalf, as the last application they should make. The king promised to consider their request, and the day following the matter was fully debated in council, in presence of his majesty, who was pleased to say, he intended an indulgence if it was at all possible. The mends of the silenced ministers in the council, whose hopes had been flattered with a variety of specious promises, were now permitted freely to state their reasons for not putting the act in execution; and they reasoned most strenuously on the impolicy and absurdity of the measure, and the fatal effects, to the nation at large, that must necessarily attend its execution. But Dr. Shelden, bishop of London, in an animated speech, declared, "That it was now too late to think of suspending a law which had occupied so much of the time and the wisdom of the legislature in enacting—A law, in obedience to which he had already ejected such of his clergy as would not comply with it; and were they now to be restored, after thus being exasperated, he must, in that case, expect to feel the weight of their resentment; and in place of maintaining his Episcopal authority amongst them, be subjected to their scorn and animosity, being thus countenanced by the court. Besides, should the sacred authority of this law be now suspended, it would render the legislature both ridiculous and contemptible; and should the pressing importunity of such disaffected people be considered a sufficient reason why they should be humored on this occasion, it would establish a precedent upon which all future malcontents would build their hopes, and maintain their claims to similar indulgence:—the obvious consequence of which would be, convulsions, and neverceasing distractions, both in church and state." It was, on these grounds, carried that no indulgence whatever should be granted. Mr. Calamy was offered a bishopric; which he refused, because he could not obtain it on the terms of the king's declaration. He preserved his temper and moderation after his ejection, and lived much retired; but going to Alder

Manbury church one day as a hearer, and the clergyman appointed to preach failing to come forward; to gratify the wishes of the people who were assembled, and prevent a disappointment, he condescended to give them a *dis coupse*, though unpremeditated. For this he was shut up in Newgate prison, by warrant from the lord mayor, as a violator of the Act of Uniformity, the great Diana of that tyrannical period.

A popish lady, passing through the city, found it almost impossible to proceed through Newgate Street for the number of coaches in waiting. Surprised at this incident, curiosity led her to inquire into the occasion. Some of the bystanders informed her, that an ejected minister, greatly beloved in the city, had been imprisoned for preaching a single sermon, and his friends were calling to pay him a visit in prison. This information so struck the lady, that she waited on the king at Whitehall, and told him the whole affair, expressing her apprehension, that such steps might alienate the affection of the city from his majesty. It was partly owing to this, that Mr. Calamy was soon released by an express order from the king. This circumstance being afterwards complained of in the House of Commons, it was signified that his release was occasioned by a deficiency of the Act itself, and not by the sole orders of his majesty. The following entry was therefore made on the journal of the House: "*Die Jovis*, 1662-63. Upon complaint made to this House, that Mr. Calamy, being committed to prison upon breach of the Act of Uniformity, was discharged upon pretense of some defect in the act—*Resolved,* That it be referred to a committee to look into the act of uniformity as to the matter in question, and see whether the same be defective, and wherein." And shortly after this, a committee was appointed to bring in the reasons of the House for advising the king to grant no toleration, with an address to his majesty; which paved the way for all that unqualified severity, and tyrannical procedure, that followed during this and the succeeding reign.

Mr. Calamy lived to see the dreadful fire of London in 1666. This awful conflagration is said to have overrun 373 acres of ground within the walls, and to have burned down 13,200 houses, and 89 parish churches, beside chapels, and that only 11 parishes within the walls were left standing. This dreadful spectacle is said to have broken Mr. Calamy's heart. He was driven through the ruins of the city in a coach, and viewing the dreadful solitude, and far spread desolation, he went home with a heavy heart, and never after left his chamber; but died in less than a month, October 1666, in the sixty-seventh year of his age.

His works are not numerous. He was one of the authors of *Smectymnuus*, formerly mentioned. He was also concerned in drawing up the *Vindication of the Presbyterial Church Government and Ministry*, and *Jus Divinum Ministerii Evangelici et Anglicani*. He has also several sermons extant:

1. England's Looking glass.

2. The Nobleman's pattern of true and real Thankfulness.

3. God's free mercy to England.

4. England's Antidote against the Plague of Civil War.

5. An Indictment against England because of her Self-murdering Divisions.

6. The great danger of Covenant refusing and Covenant breaking.

7. The Door of Truth Opened.

8. The Saint's Rest.

9. The Fragility of the Body.

10. The Monster of sinful self-seeking Anatomized.

11. A Sermon at the Funeral of the Earl of Warwick.

12. A Sermon at the Funeral of Mr. Ashe.

13. (This present work) The Godly Man's City of Refuge in the day of his distress, containing five Sermons.

Mr. Calamy's oldest son was ejected at the same time with his father; and his grandson, a dissenting divine of great eminence, is well known by his learned works.

PREFACE

Mr. Edmund Calamy, the author of the following Sermons, was an eminent Nonconformist minister. He was born in 1600, and died in 1666, pastor of a congregation in London. Many of his discourses, preached on different public and particular occasions, were published, either in consequence of the request of the hearers, or to vindicate the doctrines he preached, or, as in the present volume, with the object of benefitting his congregation. His discourses exhibit that intimate acquaintance with scripture, that clear statement of the doctrines of the gospel, and practical application of the truth to the conscience, which distinguish the labors of the Nonconformist divines of that period. Of the value of the works of that body of men, the best proof that can be given is the very general republication which has been recently made of them, and the eagerness with which they have been received by the public. The present little volume is one of the excellent publications of that time, which, though it went through many editions soon after its first appearance, has been now long extremely scarce and almost unknown. Its value, as a practical, consolatory, and experimental *Work*, is such, that the Editor considers the reprinting of it a service done to the Christian world.

J.S.
Edinburgh, 12th July, 1825.

PREFACE

Another edition of this little book has been published, because it is believed that there are those who may be quickened by it to a more diligent following of God, and confirmed in a humble, holy confidence in Him.

M.F.

Edinburgh, April, 1865.

THE GODLY MAN'S ARK

SERMON 1

Psa. 119:92, "Unless thy law had been my delights, I should then have perished in mine affliction."

This psalm, out of which my text is taken, exceeds all the other psalms, not only in length, but in excellency, so far, in the judgment of Ambrose, as the light of the sun excels the light of the moon. As the Book of Psalms is styled by Luther an epitome of the Bible, or, a little Bible; so may this psalm fitly be called an *epitome* of the Book of Psalms. It was written, as is thought, by David in the days of his banishment under Saul, but so penned, that the words of it suit the condition of all saints. It is a public storehouse of heavenly doctrines, distributing fit and convenient instructions to all the people of God; and therefore should be in no less account with those who are spiritually alive, than is the use of the sun, air and fire with those who are naturally alive. It is divided into two-and-twenty sections, according to the Hebrew alphabet, and therefore fitly called a holy alphabet for Zion's scholars, the *A B C* of godliness. Sextus Senensis calls it an alphabetical poem. The Jews are said to teach it their little children the first thing they learn, and therein they take a very right course, both in regard of the heavenly matter, and plain style fitted for all capacities. The chief scope of it is to set out the glorious excellences and perfections of the law of God, There is not a verse (except one only, say some learned men, in print, but are there deceived, but I may truly say, except the 122rd and the 90th verses) in this long psalm, wherein there is not mention made of the law of God, under the name of law, or statutes, or precepts, or testimonies, or commandments, or ordinances, or word, or promises, or ways, or judgments, of name, or righteousness, or truth, etc.

This text that I have chosen, sets out the great benefit and comfort which David found in the law of God in the time of his affliction. It kept him from perishing. "Had not thy law been my delights, I had perished in my affliction."

The word "law" is taken diversely in Scripture, sometimes for the moral law, (James 2:10); sometimes for the whole economy, polity, and regimen of Moses, for the whole Mosaic dispensation, by laws partly moral, partly judicial, partly ceremonial, (Gal. 3:33); sometimes for the five books of Moses, (Luke 24:44); sometimes for the whole doctrine of God contained in the Scriptures of the Old Testament, (John 7:49). By *law* in this place is meant, all those books of the Scripture which were written when this psalm was penned. But I shall handle it in a larger sense, as it comprehends all the books both of the Old and the New Testament. For the word "law" is sometimes also taken for the gospel, as it is Micah 4:2 and Isa. 2:3. The meaning then is, "Unless thy law," that is, "Thy Word, had been my delights, I should have perished in mine affliction."

David speaks this, Musculus says, of the distressed condition he was in when persecuted by Saul, forced to fly to the Philistines, and sometimes to hide himself in the rocks and caves of the earth. It is very likely, he says, that he had the Book of God's law with him, by the reading of which he mitigated and allayed his sorrows, and kept himself pure from communicating with the heathen in their superstitions. The Greek scholars say that David uttered these words when driven from Saul and compelled to live amongst the wicked Philistines; for he would have been allured to have communicated with them in their impieties, had he not carried about him the meditation of the Word of God. "Unless thy law had been my delights," *etc.*

In the words themselves we have two truths supposed, and one truth clearly proposed.

Two truths supposed:
1. That the dearest of God's saints are subject to many great and tedious afflictions.
2. That the Word of God is the saints' darling and delights.

One truth clearly proposed:
That the law of God delighted in, is the afflicted saint's antidote against ruin and destruction.

Two truths supposed:

The first is this—

Doctrine: 1: *That the best of God's saints are in this life subject to many great and tedious afflictions.*

David was a man after God's own heart, and yet he was a man made up of troubles of all sorts and sizes, insomuch as he professes of himself, (Psa. 69:1-3), "Save me, O God, for the waters are come in to my soul; I sink in deep mire, where there is no standing; I am come into deep waters, where the floods overflow me; I am weary of my crying, my throat is dried, mine eyes fail while I wait for my God." And in this text he professes that his afflictions were so great, that he must necessarily have perished under them had he not been sustained by the powerful comforts he fetched out of the Word. There is an emphasis in the word "then." "I should *then* have perished;" that is, long before this time; "then," when I was afflicted, "then" I should have perished. Junius and

Tremelius translate it, *I should long ago have perished.* Job was a man eminent for godliness, and yet as equally eminent for afflictions. No, Jesus Christ himself was a man of sorrows, (Isa. 53:3). Insomuch as that it is truly said, "God had one Son without sin, but no son without sorrow."

This our dear sister, at whose funeral we are met, was a woman full of many and great afflictions, which (no doubt) would have quite drowned and swallowed her up, had not the Word of God supported her; therefore it was that she desired that this text might be the subject of her funeral sermon.

Question. But why does God afflict His own children with such variety of long and great afflictions?

Answer. 1. God does not do this because He hates them, but because He loves them, "For whom the Lord loves he chasteneth," *etc.*, (Heb. 12:6). Did the Lord hate them? If he did then He would suffer them to go merrily *to hell.* There is no surer sign of God's reprobating anger, than to suffer a man to prosper in wicked courses. God threatens this as the greatest punishment, not to punish them now, (Hos. 4:14). And therefore because God loves His children He chastises them in this world that they may not be condemned in the world to come, (1 Cor. 11:32).

2. God does not do this because He would hurt them, but for their good. The good figs were sent into captivity for their good, (Jer. 24:5). He for our profit, *etc.* (Heb. 12:10). God has very gracious and merciful ends and aims in afflicting His people. Give me leave here to enlarge my discourse, and to give you an account of some of these *divine* aims.

I. God's design is to teach us to know Him and to trust in Him, and to know ourselves. It is a true saying of Luther's—*The school of affliction is a school of instruction.* God's rods, when sanctified, are powerful sermons to teach us,

1. To *know* God. "And this is life eternal to know Him," (John 17:3). It is said of Manasseh, (2, Chron. 33:13), "Then Manasseh knew that the Lord he was God"—this happened when he was caught among the thorns, bound with chains, and carried to Babylon. Before that time he did not know the Lord. Afflictions teach us to know God, and not only in His power and greatness, in His anger and hatred against sin, but also in His goodness and mercy. For God so sweetens the bitter cup of affliction, that a child of God many times tastes more of God's love in one month's affliction than in many years of prosperity, (1 Cor. 1:4-5, 8:4). Add to this, afflictions teach us to know God *experimentally* and *affectionately.* So, this is to know Him, as to love and fear Him, and to fly to Him as our rock and hiding-place in the day of our distress. It is said, (Song of Songs 3:1), "By night I sought him whom my soul loves," *etc.* Some by the word "night" understand the night of Divine desertion. From the words, Gilbertus has this saying— *He that seeks after God in the night of adversity, does not seek to see Him and know Him formally and superficially, but to embrace Him, and to love Him really and cordially.* And, therefore, the Church never left until she had found Christ, and when she had found Him, she held Him, and would not let Him go, (Song of Songs 3:2-4).

2. Not only to know God, but also to *trust* in Him, (2 Cor. 1:9), "We had the sentence of death in ourselves, that we should not trust in ourselves, but in God, which raiseth the dead." Note here, (1). That an apostle is often in time of prosperity to trust in himself; (2). That God brings His children to the gates of death, that they might learn not to trust in themselves, but in God, who raises the dead, that is, from a dead and desperate condition.

3. Not only to know God, but to know ourselves, which two are the chief parts of Christian religion. It is said of the prodigal, that when he was in adversity, then he "came to himself"—(Luke 15:17), "And when he came to himself." He was spiritually distracted when he was in prosperity. Afflictions teach us to know that we are but men, according to that of David, as in Psa. 9:20, "Put them in fear, O Lord, that they may know themselves to be but men." Caligula and Domitian, emperors of Rome, who in prosperity would be called *gods*, when it thundered from heaven were so terrified, that then they knew they were but men. In prosperity we forget our mortality. Adversity causes us to know, not only that we are men, but frail men, that God has us between His hands, (as it is Ezek. 21:17), and can as easily crush us as we crush moths; that we are in God's hands, as the clay in the hands of the potter; that He has an absolute sovereignty over us, and that we depend on Him for our being, well-being, and eternal being. These things we know feelingly and practically in the day of affliction. And it should concern us greatly to know these things, and to know them powerfully, for this will make us stand in awe of God, and study to serve and please Him. He that depends on a man for his livelihood, knowing that he has him at an advantage, and can easily undo him, will certainly endeavor to comply with him, and to obtain his favor. The ground of all service and obedience is dependence. And did we really and experimentally know our dependence on God, and the advantages He has over us, we could not, we would not but comply with Him, and labor above all things to gain His love and favor.

II. God's aim in afflicting His children, is either to keep them from sin, or, when they have sinned, to bring them to repentance for it, and from it.

1. To keep them from sin. This made Him send an

angel of Satan to buffet Paul, lest he should be lifted up in pride, and exalted above measure, (2 Cor. 12:7).

2. *The second design of God afflicting his children.* The second design is that when they have sinned, God brings them to repentance for it, and from it. God brings His children low, not to trample on them, but to make them low in their own eyes, and to humble them for sin, (Deut. 8:2). God brings them into the deep waters, not to drown them, but to wash and cleanse them. Isa. 27:9 says, "By this shall the iniquity of Jacob be purged; and this is all the fruit to take away sin," *etc.* Afflictions, when sanctified, are *divine hammers* to break, and as Moses' rod, to cleave our rocky hearts in pieces.

(1). They open the eyes to see sin.

When the brethren of Joseph were in adversity then they saw, and not before, the greatness of their sin in selling their brother, (Gen. 52:21).

(a). They open the ear to discipline.

In prosperity we turn a deaf ear to the voice of the Charmer, though He charm never so wisely. But adversity opens the ear, and causes us to attend. When God spoke on Mount Sinai in a terrible manner, then the people said to Moses: "Speak thou to us all that the Lord our God shall speak to thee, and we will hear it and do it," (Deut. 5:27). Memorable is that text in Jer. 2:2, "A wild ass used to the wilderness, that snuffeth up the wind at her pleasure, in her occasion who can turn her away? All they that seek her will not weary themselves, in her mouth they shall find her;"—"in her month," that is, when she is great with young, and near her time. A wicked man in the day of his prosperity is like a wild ass used to the wilderness: he snuffs at any that shall reprove him, he is of an uncircumcised ear, and a rebellious heart; but in his month, that is, when he is bent with afflictions, then he will be easily found; this will open his ear to discipline.

(3). They will open the mouth to confess sin, (Judges 10:15).

(4). They will command us to depart from iniquity, (Job 36:8-10).

Afflictions are God's furnaces to purge out the dross of our sins; God's files to pare off our spiritual rust; God's fans to winnow out our chaff. In prosperity we gather much soil, but adversity purges and purifies us. This is its proper work, to work out unrighteousness, (Dan. 11:35, 12:10).

3. The third design. God's end is not only to keep us from sin, but to make us holy and righteous; therefore it is said, (Isa. 26:9), "When thy judgments are in the earth, the inhabitants of the world will learn righteousness." And Heb. 12:10, "He for our profit, that we may be partakers of his holiness." As the waters that drowned the old world did not hurt the ark of Noah, but held it up above the earth, and as they increased, so the ark was lifted up nearer and nearer to heaven; so afflictions, when sanctified, do not prejudice the saints of God, but lift them up nearer to God in holiness and heavenly-mindedness.

4. The fourth design. God's design in afflicting His children, is to make the world bitter to them and Christ sweet.

(1). To embitter the world. There are two lame legs on which all worldly things stand, *uncertainty* and *insufficiency*. All earthly things are like the earth, founded on nothing; they are like heaps made of wax that quickly melts away. Riches and honors, wife and children, have wings and fly away; they are like Absalom's mule, they will fail us when we have most need of them. They may puff up the soul, but they cannot satisfy it. They are all *vanity and vexation of spirit*, so says the preacher; but most people in time of health will not believe these things; but when some great sickness comes upon them, this is as a real sermon, to make out the truth of them; then they see that a velvet slipper cannot cure the gout, nor a golden cap the headache; that riches do not avail in the day of wrath, (Prov. 10:4); and this embitters the world.

(a). To make Christ sweet and precious. When Christ and His disciples were in a ship together, (Matt. 8:25), it is said that Christ was asleep; and as long as the sea was calm His disciples suffered Him to sleep, but when they were ready to be drowned, then they awoke Christ, and said, "Master, save us, we perish." Even the best of saints when fatted with outward plenty and abundance, are prone to suffer Christ to lie asleep within them, and so neglect the lively actings of faith on Christ; but when the storms of affliction and outward calamity begin to arise, and they are ready to be overwhelmed with distress, then—none but Christ—none but Christ.

5. God's design in afflicting His children is to prove and improve their graces.

(1). To prove their graces, (Rev. 2:10, Deut. 8:2), to prove the truth and the strength of them. 1. The truth and sincerity of their graces. For this cause He loaded Job with afflictions, to try whether he served God for his camels and oxen, or for *love* to God. As Solomon's sword tried the true mother from the false, so the sword of affliction discovers the sincere Christian from the hypocrite. Distresses are *divine* touchstones to try whether we are true or counterfeit saints. That grace is true which on trial is found true. 2. To try the strength of our graces. For it requires a strong faith to endure great afflictions. That faith which will suffice for a little affliction, will not suffice for a great one. Peter had faith enough to come to Christ on the sea, but as soon as the storm began to arise his faith began to fail, and Christ said, "Why art thou afraid, O thou of little faith?" (Matt.

14:30-31). It must be a strong faith that must keep us from sinking in the day of great distress.

(2). To improve our graces. It is reported of the lioness that she leaves her young ones until they have almost killed themselves with roaring and howling, and then at the last gasp she relieves them, and by this means they become more courageous. So God brings His children into the deeps, and suffers Jonah to be three days and three nights in the belly of the whale, and David to cry until his throat was dry, (Psa. 60:3), and suffers His apostles to be all the night in a great storm until the fourth watch, and then He comes and rebukes the winds, and by this means He mightily increases their patience and dependence on God, and their faith in Christ. As the palm tree, the more it is depressed, the higher, stronger, and more fruitful it grows; so does the grace of God's people.

Lastly, God's aim in afflicting His people is to put an edge on their prayers, and all their other holy services.

(1.). On prayer. What a famous prayer Manasseh made when he was under his iron chains. It is three times mentioned, (2 Chron. 33:13, 18, 19). When Paul was struck off his horse, and struck with blindness, then he prayed to purpose. Therefore it is said, (Acts 9:11), "Behold he prays! "In prosperity we pray heavily and drowsily, but adversity adds wings to our prayers, (Isa. 26:16). The very heathen mariners cried aloud to God in a storm. It is an ordinary saying, There are no sailors so wicked but they will pray when in a great storm.

(2). On preaching. Prosperity makes a glutton of the spiritual appetite, adversity whets it.

(3). On a sacrament. How sweet is a sacrament to a true saint after a long and great sickness? It makes God and the Word of God precious. If God sets our cornfields on fire, (as Absalom did Joab's), then He shall be sure to cause us to come running to Him. And how sweet is a text of Scripture to a child of God in the hour of his distress!

By all this it appears that God afflicts His children not to hurt them, but to help them, and that God has many glorious and gracious ends and aims in afflicting of them. Therefore it is that David says of himself in verse 71 of this psalm, "It is good for me that I have been afflicted, that I might learn thy statutes." He never said, *It is good for me that I have been in prosperity*, but he rather says the contrary in the 67th verse, "Before I was afflicted, I went astray, but now I have kept thy word." God's people will bless God as much, if not more, in heaven for their adversity, than for their prosperity.

Use 1. Let us not pass rash censures on people under great afflictions. Do not say, *Such a woman is a greater sinner than others*, because she is more afflicted. This was the fault of Job's friends, and God expresses His anger against them for it, (Job 52:7), "My wrath is kindled against thee, and thy two friends, for you have not spoken the thing that is right," *etc.* This was the fault of the barbarians, (Acts 28:4), "When they saw the venomous beast hang on the hand of Paul, they said among themselves, No doubt this man is a murderer," *etc.* But remember they were *barbarians.* It is a sign of a barbarian, not of a Christian, to pass a rash judgment on people in affliction. "Think you," says Christ, "that those eighteen on whom the tower in Siloam fell and slew them, that they were sinners above all men that dwelt in Jerusalem? I tell you, Nay; but except you repent, ye shall all likewise perish," (Luke 13:4, 5). You must think that they which have a gallstone and gout in extremity, that have cancers in their faces and breasts, are greater sinners than others? I tell you *No, etc.* For my part, if I would censure any, it should be such as live wickedly, and meet with no affliction. These have the *black brand of reprobation* on them; these are men designed to damnation. Ambrose would not tarry a night in the house of a gentleman that had never in all his life been afflicted, for fear, as he said, lest some great and sudden judgment should come upon him. But when I see a godly woman afflicted, then I say, *This is not so much for her sin, as for her trial;* this is not to hurt her, but to *teach her to know God,* and *to know herself,* to break her heart for sin, and from sin, to make the world bitter, and Christ sweet. God has put her into the fire of affliction to refine her, and make her a vessel fit for His use. God is striking her with the hammer of affliction, that she may be squared, and made ready to be laid in the heavenly Jerusalem.

Use 2. Here is rich comfort to the children of God under the greatest afflictions. For the best of saints are subject to the worst afflictions. This is the lot of all God's children, Christ himself not excepted. Afflictions, indeed, considered in their own nature, are evil things, and so are called, (Amos 5:13). They are part of the curse due to sin, the fruit of God's revenging wrath; they are as a biting and stinging serpent; and to a wicked man, remaining wicked, *they are the beginning of hell.* Unsanctified afflictions parboil a wicked man for hell and damnation. But now to a child of God, they have lost both their name and nature, they are not punishments properly, but chastisements; they are not satisfactory, but castigatory. Jesus Christ has taken away the sting of these serpents; they are not fiery but brazen serpents; they have a healing, not a hurting power. Christ has removed the curse and bitterness of them. As the wood sweetened the waters of Marah, (Exod. 15:25), so Christ's cross has sweetened the bitterness of afflictions.

There are eight comfortable considerations to cheer the heart of a child of God in the day of his distress.

1. God never afflicts His people but out of pure

necessity, (1 Pet 2:6), "Though now for a season, if need be, ye are in heaviness,"—as a most loving father never corrects his child, but when he is forced to it. He willingly provides for his child, but punishes him unwillingly; so God freely loads with His blessings, but He never chastises His children but when forced to it; therefore He says expressly, (Lam. 3:23), "He does not afflict willingly," (Isa. 27:1), "Fury is not in me." It is we that put thunderbolts in God's hand. If the sun did not first draw up the vapors from the earth, there would never be any thundering or lightning. God would never thunder from heaven with His judgments, if our sins did not first cry to heaven for punishment. As Christ whipped the sellers of oxen and sheep out of the temple with a whip made, in all probability, of their own cords; so God never scourges us, but it is with a whip made out of our own sins; (Prov. 5:22; Rom. 2:5), "Thou treasurest up to thyself," *etc.* God has a double treasure, a treasure of *mercy*, and a treasure of *wrath*; His treasure of mercy is always full, but His treasure of wrath is empty, until we fill it by our sins. And therefore when God punishes His children, He calls it a strange work, and a strange act, (Isa. 28:21). It is observed of the bee that it never stings but when provoked. I am sure that God never afflicts His children but out of pure necessity.

2. Not only out of pure necessity, but out of true and real love; as I have showed, (Heb. 12:6-8).

Objection. Do not Divine afflictions proceed out of anger? Was not God angry with Moses for speaking unadvisedly with his lips? And angry with David for his adultery, and there afflicted both of them? *Answer.* This anger was a fatherly anger rooted in love. As it is a great punishment for God sometimes not to punish, (Isa. 1:5; Hos. 4:14), so it is a great mercy sometimes for God to withdraw His mercy.

3. Afflictions are a part of Divine predestination.

That God which has elected us to salvation has also elected us to afflictions, (1 Thes. 1:2), "That no man should be moved by these afflictions; for you yourselves know that we are appointed thereto." The same love with which God elects us, and bestows Christ and His Spirit on us, with the very same love He afflicts us.

4. They are part of the gracious covenant which God has made with His people, (Psa. 89:31-33), in which words we have three things considerable.

(1). A supposition of sin. If his children *forsake my law, etc.* For sin is always the cause without which God will never chastise us, and for the most part it is the cause for which He does chastise us.

(2). We have a gracious promise: "Then I will visit their transgression with the rod, and their iniquity with stripes."

(3). We have a merciful qualification, "Nevertheless my loving-kindness will I not utterly take from him, nor suffer my faithfulness to fail; my covenant will I not break," *etc.* Afflictions are not only mercies, but covenant mercies; therefore David says, (Psa. 119:75), "And that thou in faithfulness hast afflicted me." God would be unfaithful if He did not afflict His children.

5. Consider that afflictions are part of the saint's blessedness. (Job 5:17), "Behold! happy is the man whom God correcteth," *etc.* "Behold," says Eliphaz, and we had need behold, and consider it, for there are few that believe it; and yet it is most true, that afflictions, when sanctified, when they are not only corrections, but instructions, then they are evidences that we are in a blessed condition. Eliphaz's saying must be interpreted by what David says, (Psa. 94:12), "Blessed is the man whom thou chastisest, O Lord, and teachest out of thy law." It is not correction simply, but correction joined with instruction, which entitles us to happiness. Job even while he was on the dunghill, wonders that God

should set His heart so much on him, as to visit him every morning, and to try him every moment, (Job 7:17-18). Job on the dunghill was happier than Adam in Paradise: Adam in Paradise was conquered by the devil; but Job on the dunghill overcame the devil. Lazarus in his rags was happier than Dives in his robes; Philpot in his coal-house, than Bonner in his palace; and godly Mr Whitaker on his bed of pain, than a wicked man on his bed of down. There were many in Christ's time who would never have known Him, or come to Him, had it not been for their bodily diseases.

6. Consider the gracious and merciful ends, aims, and designs that God has in afflicting His people; what these are ye have heard already.

7. The sweet and precious promises, which He has made to His children in the day of their adversity, to comfort them and support them; what these are you shall hear afterwards.

8. Consider that all afflictions shall work at last for the good of God's children, (Rom. 8:28). Though they are not good in themselves, yet they shall turn to their good. God beats His children, as we do our clothes in the sun, only to beat out the moths; God puts them into the fiery furnace, not to hurt them, but only to untie the bonds of their sins; as He dealt with the three children, (Dan. 3:25). God will either deliver them out of their afflictions, or send them to heaven by them; wherefore comfort one another with these words.

Use 3. If the best of saints are subject in this life to many great and tedious afflictions, then let us

1. Expect afflictions.
2. Prepare for them.
3. Improve them.

1. *Let us expect afflictions*, for Christ has said expressly, (John 16:33), "In the world ye shall have tribulation." There is in every child of God—

(1). A sufficient foundation, for God to build a house of correction on. There is sin enough to deserve affliction.

(2.) There are motives sufficient to prevail with God to chastise them when they sin against Him; some of these you have heard already, let me add one more: Because He is more dishonored by the sins of His own children than by the sins of wicked men. As it is a greater discredit to an earthly father when his own children, than when other men's children, live wickedly; so it is a greater disparagement to our heavenly Father when His own sons and daughters, than when the devil's children transgress His law: and, therefore, God will chastise them sooner, surer, and more than others. 1. Sooner, (Rom. 2:9), a Tribulation and anguish on every soul of man that does evil, "of the Jew first, and also of the Gentile." First the Jew, and then the Gentile. 2. Surer than others: (Amos 3:2), "You only have I known of all the families of the earth, therefore I will punish you for all your iniquities." 3. More than others, (Lam. 4:6), "The punishment of the iniquity of the daughter of my people is greater than the punishment of the sin of Sodom," *etc.*; (Dan. 9:12), "Under the whole heaven has not been done, as has been done on Jerusalem."

(3.) There is sufficient necessity to provoke God to afflict them. It is needful that the wheat be winnowed, that so the chaff may be separated from it. It is needful that the wind blow on the wheat, to cleanse it, and that gold be put into the furnace, to purge and purify it. When the sheep of Christ are divided one from the other in judgment and afflictions, when separated in doctrine, worship, and discipline, it is very needful that God should send afflictions and distresses, which may be, as the shepherd's dog, very serviceable and instrumental to unite them together, and to gather them into one sheepfold; and therefore let the saints of God expect afflictions.

2. God's people are to *prepare for afflictions*. Let us prepare and provide against the day of tribulation. Let us provide,

(1.) A stock of graces. For sickness is a time to spend grace, but not to get grace. A Christian in sickness without grace is like a soldier in war without armor; like a house in stormy weather without a foundation; and like the men of the old world, when ready to be drowned, without an ark. Woe be to that person that has his graces to get when he should use them! And therefore if we would be comforted in the day of tribulation, we must provide beforehand a furniture of graces.

1st. A true faith, (for a painted faith will avail no more than a painted helmet, or a painted ship), and not only a true but also a strong faith. A little faith will faint under great afflictions; when the winds began to blow fiercely Peter's little faith began to fail, (Matt. 14:30).

2nd. A great measure of patience, to enable us to wait quietly and contentedly, until God comes in with help, for many times He tarries until the fourth watch of the night, as He did in Matt. 14:25; and therefore we have need of patience to keep us from murmuring or repining.

3rd. A great stock of self-denial, humility, repentance, contempt of the world, and heavenly-mindedness, He that is furnished with grace in an evil hour, will be as safe and secure as Noah was in the ark in the time of the deluge, or as those were who had sufficiency of corn in the time of the seven years' pain in Egypt.

(2.) A stock of assurance of salvation. For though a man has never so much grace, yet if he wants the assurance of it, he cannot receive any comfort by it in the day of his distress. Jacob was not at all quieted in his spirit for Joseph's being alive until he came to know of it; and therefore we must not only provide grace, but the assurance of grace, that we may be able to say with confidence, as Job did on the dunghill, (Job 19:25), "I know that my Redeemer liveth;" and with the holy apostle, (Rem. 8:38), "I am persuaded, that neither death, nor life, nor angels, nor principalities, nor powers, nor things present, nor things to come, nor height, nor depth, nor any other creature, shall be able to separate us from the love of God, which is in Christ Jesus our Lord." That man who has got a Scripture assurance of his salvation, will be more than a conqueror in the day of his distress.

(3.) A stock of divine experiences. Happy is that man that stores up in his heart all the former experiences he has had of God's love and mercy towards him, and knows how to argue from them in the day of calamity. So did Moses in his prayer to God, (Numb. 14:19), "Pardon, I beseech thee, the iniquity of this people, according to the greatness of thy mercy, and as you have forgiven this people from Egypt, even until now!" Because God had forgiven them, therefore Moses entreats Him to forgive them; this argument is drawn from former experience. And so David encourages himself, (1 Sam. 17:37), "The Lord has delivered me out of the paw of the lion, and out of the paw of the bear, and he will deliver me out of the hand of this Philistine." So also Paul reasons, (a Cor. 1:10), "Who delivered us from so great a death, and does deliver, and in whom we trust that he will yet deliver us." Divine experiences are the saints' great encouragements in the day of affliction. Blessed is the man that has his quiver full of these arrows.

(4.) A stock of sermons. We must do with sermons as the tradesmen do with the money they get; some of it they lay out for their present use, and some of it they lay up against the time of sickness. That man is an ill husband, and an unthrifty tradesman that makes no provision for old age or for an evil day; and that man is an unprofitable hearer of the word, who does not stock and store himself with sermons, whereby he may be comforted in the hour of affliction. And therefore the prophet Isaiah advises us, (Isa. 42:23), "To hear for the time to come," or, as it is in the Hebrew, "for the after-time." Sermons are not only to be heard for our present use, but to be laid up for *after-times*, that when we lie on our sick-beds, and cannot hear sermons, we may then live on the sermons we have heard.

(5). And lastly, we must prepare and provide a stock of Scripture promises, which will be as so many reviving cordials, to cheer us, and as so many spiritual anchors, to uphold us from perishing in the day of our tribulation. What these promises are you shall hear afterwards. These upheld David in the hour of his distress, and therefore he says in the text, "Unless thy law had been my delight, I had perished in mine affliction." If this our dear sister had not had this stock, she had been quite overwhelmed under the grievousness of her tormenting pains. Be wise, therefore, O you saints of God, and prepare these five provisions in the time of health, that so you may live joyfully in the time of sickness.

3. As we must expect and provide for afflictions, so also we must labor, when afflicted, to improve them for our spiritual benefit and advantage. We must pray more for the sanctification of them, than for their removal. It was not the staff of Elisha that revived the dead child, but Elisha himself. It was not the troubling of the waters of the pool of Bethesda that made them healing, but the coming down of the angel. It was not the clay and spit that cured the eyes of the blind, but Christ's anointing them with it. It was not the cloak of Elijah that divided the waters, but the God of Elijah. Troubles,

strokes, blows, afflictions, and distresses will do us no good unless the Lord be pleased to make them effectual; and therefore let us pray to God that He would give us grace together with our afflictions; that He would add instruction to His correction, that He would make us good scholars in the school of afflictions, and enable us to take out all those excellent lessons which He would have us to learn in it, that thereby he may come to know God more powerfully and experimentally, and to know ourselves and our own family, and our absolute dependence on God more effectually; that thereby we may be more purified and refined, that the wind of temptation may cleanse us from the chaff of our corruption; that we may learn righteousness by God's judgments, and be made partakers of His holiness. Such a good scholar was Manasseh; he got more good by his iron chain than by his golden chain. Such another was the prodigal child, who was happier amongst the swine than when in his father's house. Such was Paul; his being stricken down to the ground, raised him up to heaven; by the blindness of his body his soul received sight; and he was turned from a persecuting Saul to a persecuted Paul. Such another was David, who professes of himself that it was good for him that he was afflicted; and such scholars ought we to be.

There are some that are arrant dunces in this school, that are like to the bush which Moses saw, which burned with fire, but was not consumed; the fire did not consume the thorny bush. Many such thorny sinners are burnt up with the fire of divine afflictions, but their sins are not consumed. Of these the prophets complain, (Amos 4:6-12), "Yet they have not returned," *etc.*; (Jer. 5:3), "You have stricken them, but they have not grieved; you have consumed them, but they have refused to receive correction; they have made their faces harder than a rock, they have refused to return." Rocks and stones, by hewing and polishing, may be made fit for a building; but there are some men who by no afflictions will be amended. The mountains melt at the presence of the Lord, and the rocks rend asunder when He is angry. But there are some that have made their faces harder than the rocks and the mountains, and are not at all affected with God's anger.

There are others that are the worse for their afflictions; like the smith's anvil, the more they are stricken, the harder they are: such a one was King Ahaz, (2 Chron. 28:20), "In the time of his distress he did trespass yet more against the Lord." There is a brand put on him. This is that King Ahaz, that wicked King Ahaz, that reprobate King Ahaz. As pearls put in vinegar lose their color and beauty, so many, when under God's hand, lose all their glory and excellency, and begin to distrust God's providence, to call His justice into question, to murmur and repine against God's dealings, and to use unlawful means for their deliverance. Of these the prophet Isaiah complains, (Isa. 1:5), "Why should you be stricken any more? Ye will revolt more and more." Such was Ahaziah, (2 Kings 1:2), that sought for help from Beelzebub, the god of Ekron; and such was Saul, who sought to the witch of Endor for health in the day of his distress.

Both of these sorts are in a sad and miserable condition: for God has two furnaces, the furnace of affliction and the furnace of hell-fire. If the first furnace will not purge us, the second will everlastingly consume us. As the Roman consuls had a man appointed to go before them, carrying a rod and an axe; a rod for the punishing of corrigible offenders, an axe for the destruction of incorrigible; so God has His rod and His axe, His pruning-knife and His chopping-knife, His warning piece and His murdering-pieces. Afflictions are His rods to correct us for our sin; His pruning-knife, to pare off our luxuriant branches; His warning-pieces to call on us to repent.

But if His warning-pieces will do us no good, we must expect His murdering-pieces. If His pruning-knife will not amend us, His chopping-knife will confound us. If His rods will not reclaim us, then His axe will hew us down, and cast us into everlasting fire. God has three houses, the house of instruction, of correction, and of destruction. The place where God's people meet to hear His Word, is His house of instruction; and if we profit in this house, He will never carry us to the house of correction. But if we be stubborn and rebellious in the house of instruction, then He will send us to the house of correction; and if we profit in this house, He will never send us into the house of destruction: but if we continue incorrigible in the house of correction, He will inevitably send us to the house of destruction, that is, to hell-fire.

And, therefore, whensoever God brings us into the school of affliction, let us labor to be good scholars in it, and to answer all those ends, aims, and designs which God has in afflicting of us. Let us pray to God that our afflictions may be divine hammers to break our hearts for sin, and from sin; may make the world bitter, and Christ more precious; may prove and improve our graces, and may put an edge on all holy duties.

There are two things I would have you in an especial manner to labor after:—

1. Labor, when afflicted, to know the meaning of God's rod.

2. That the good you get by afflictions may abide on you after your recovery from them.

1. You must labor to know the Gods people meaning of God's rod, and what particular errand is which He has to you in the day of your distresses; you must do as David did, (2 Sam. 21:1).

He inquired of the Lord to know the reason why

He sent a famine amongst them. So must you, you must pray as Job does, (Job 10:2), "Show me, O Lord, wherefore thou contendest with me?" When the cause of a disease is found out, it is half cured. Your great care, therefore, must be to study to know the particular cause and reason why God turns your prosperity into adversity. The prophet Micah tells us, (Micah 6:9), "That the rod has a voice," and that the "man of wisdom shall see God's name on it." There is a great measure of spiritual art and wisdom required to enable a man to hear this voice, and to understand the language of it. A spiritual fool cannot do it.

Question. What must we do, that we may understand the voice of the rod? *Answer.* You must know that the rod of God ordinarily speaks three languages; it is sent for correction for sin, for the trial and exercise of grace, and for instruction in holiness. Sometimes, indeed, it is sent only for trial and instruction, and not at all for sin. On this account was Job afflicted, and the blind man, (Job 9:3). But for the most part it has a threefold voice; it is appointed for instruction, probation, and also for correction, (Lam. 3:39; Isa. 42:24; Luke 1:20; 1 Cor. 11:30).

Question. How shall a man know whether his afflictions are only for trial and instruction, and not at all for sin? *Answer.* The safest and best way for a Christian in this case, is to believe that all his afflictions are both for trial and instruction, and also for sin: indeed, when he sees another man, who is very godly, grievously diseased, he may charitably believe that this is for his trial, and not for his sin; but when it is his own case, then (as Dr. Ames says most excellently) "It is most equal, most safe, and most acceptable to God, to have an eye on our sins, which have either directly procured them, or at least deserved them. For though afflictions are not always sent directly and especially for sin, yet sin is the original and foundation of all afflictions."

Question. What course must we take to find out what that sin is in particular for which God corrects us? *Answer.* 1. Sometimes we may read our sin in our punishment. Adonibezek, though a heathen king, did this, (Judg. 1:7), "Threescore and ten kings, having their thumbs and their great toes cut off, gathered their meat under my table; as I have done, so God has requited me." I read of holy Ephraim, that he was converted by the suitableness of his affliction to the sin he had committed, for he saw clearly that his misery came not by chance, but from God immediately, and for sin. As a man may sometimes gather the disease of the patient by observing the physician's bill; so he may guess at his sin by considering his punishment.

2. Consider what that sin is for which your conscience does most of all accuse thee. Conscience is God's vicegerent, His bosom-preacher. And when we slight the voice of conscience, God seconds it with the voice of His rod, which speaks the very same language that conscience does.

3. Consider what is the sin of your complexion and constitution, what is your beloved sin? What is that sin to which you are most of all inclined; and if that sin prevail over you, and you cannot say with David, (Psa. 18:23), "I have kept myself from mine iniquity," it is very probable that for the subduing of that sin you are corrected of God.

4. If ever you have been at the gates of death, despairing of life, consider what that sin was which did then most of all trouble and perplex your conscience; or if you have ever been in a dream, supposing yourself to be dying, and breathing out your last breathe, what was that sin which did then most of all affright you: it is very likely that God, by afflicting you, intends to get that sin more conquered and mortified.

5. Consider what those sins are for which your godly minister, under whose care you live, reproves you, and of which your true and real friends accuse you; for, if you have slighted the voice of your faithful minister and friends, surely God, out of His love to thee, follows their advice with the voice of His rod, that thereby He may open your ear to discipline, and command you to depart from those iniquities.

But if you cannot find out that particular sin, for which God afflicts you, labor to repent of every sin, and then you will be sure to repent of that sin. If you cannot find out the bee that stings you, pull down the whole hive; or the thorn that pricks you, pull down the whole hedge. Do that out of wisdom, which Herod did out of malice, who because he could not find out the babe Jesus, killed all the children in Bethlehem, from two years old and under, that so he might be sure to kill Jesus. Let us seek the utter ruin and death of all our sins, and then we shall be sure to destroy that sin for which God afflicts us; and when the cause is removed, the disease will forthwith be cured, and the Almighty pacified and reconciled to us.

4. Let us labor that the good we reap by our afflictions may abide on us after our recovery from them. There are very many who, while they are under the rod, seem to be very penitent, and purpose and promise to amend their lives, but as soon as the rod is removed they return like the dog to the vomit, *etc.* Such was Pharaoh; while he was plagued he confessed his sin, and prayed for pardon, but as soon as the judgment was gone he hardened his heart. Such were the Israelites, (Psa. 78:34-37), "They were not steadfast, they turned back." Just like a truant schoolboy, who while his master is whipping him, will promise anything, but when it is done forgets presently to do what he promised; or like water, which while it is on the fire is very hot, but as

soon as ever it is taken off the fire presently grows cold. I knew a man who in the time of his sickness was so terrified in his conscience for his sins that he made the very bed to shake on which he lay, and cried out all night long, "I am damned, I am damned," and made many and great protestations of amendment of life, if God would be pleased to recover him. In a little while he did recover; and being recovered, was as bad and as wicked as ever before.

And therefore let us labor that the good we get by our afflictions may not vanish away with them, but may abide on us after we are recovered, that we may be able to say with David, "It is good for me that I was afflicted;" not only that I am, but that I was; David praises God in health for the good he had got in sickness, and which still abode with him. Let us say with the same prophet, (Psa. 66:13, 14), "I will go into thy house with burnt-offerings; I will pay thee my vows which my lips have uttered, and my mouth have spoken, when I was in trouble." Let us pray to God that His affliction may not only skin over our spiritual diseases, and expose our sins, but mortify them, and so change our natures that we may never return to folly. I will conclude this point with a famous saying of Plinius Secundus, worthy to be written in letters of gold. A friend writes to him, and entreats him to give him advice how to frame his life, so as he might live as becomes a good man. He returns him this answer: *I will not prescribe many rules; there is this one only which I commend to thee above all other—Let us labor to continue and persevere to be such, when we are well, as we purpose and promise to ourselves to be when we are sick. There is hardly any man so wicked but he will in sickness make many and great promises of a new life and of universal reformation if God would restore him.* Now then, if we not only be such, but continue to be such when restored, as we promise to be when sick, then we shall be excellent scholars in the school of affliction, and God will either, as I have already said, deliver us out of affliction, or send us to heaven by affliction. So much for the first truth supposed.

SERMON 2

Psa. 119:92, "Unless thy law had been my delights, I should then have perished in mine affliction."

Now I come to speak of the second truth supposed in the text.

The second truth is that *the Word of God is the saint's darling and delight.* Not only their delight, but, in the plural number, their *delights;* that is, as our annotations say, *a saint does greatly delight in God's law,* or as Junius, *All the delight of a saint is in God's law,* God's Word is the center of his delights. Many were the troubles and sorrows of David's life, but against them all he found as many comforts and delectations in God's Word; therefore he says, (verse 29), "Thy testimonies are my delights," *etc.*; and, (verse 143), "Trouble and anguish have taken hold on me; yet thy commandments are my delights." And in the text, "Unless thy law had been my delights," *etc.* While others delight in vanity and iniquity, while others take pleasure in hunting, hawking, carding, dicing, eating and drinking, the saints of God can say with Austin—*Thy Holy Scriptures are my holy delights.*

Question. Why do the saints of God take such delight in the law of God? *Answer.* 1. Because they are spiritually enlightened; their eyes are opened to behold the glory and beauty, and to understand the deep mysteries of the law; therefore David prays, (verse 18), "Open thou mine eyes, that I may behold wondrous things out of thy law." As the apostle says of the Jews, (2 Cor. 3:14, 15, 18), "That to this day there is a veil over their hearts when Moses is read; and when they shall return to the Lord, this veil shall be removed." So it is with Christians; when a wicked man reads the Word, there is a veil over his eyes, and over his heart, and over the Scriptures." The god of this world has so "blinded his eyes" that he cannot behold the beauty and glory of them; but the true saint has this veil removed; Christ has anointed his eyes with spiritual eye-salve; he sees a surpassing excellency in the Word of God, and, therefore, cannot but delight in it.

2. Because they are not only enlightened, but regenerated. And as children new born by the instinct of nature, have a natural appetite to milk for conservation of their life; so the new-born saint, by the instinct of grace, has a spiritual appetite to the Word of God; according to that of Saint Peter, (1 Pet. 2:2), "As new-born babes, desire the sincere milk of the word, that you may grow thereby." The Word of God is the saint's food; and as it is impossible for a child unborn to desire food, so for a man unregenerated to hunger after, and take true pleasure in the Word; and as it is impossible for a new-born child not to delight in milk, so it is as impossible for a regenerate Christian not to delight in the law of God.

3. Because a true saint has the law of God written in his heart, according to that precious promise of the covenant of grace, (Jer. 31:33), "I will put my law in their inward parts, and write it in their hearts." A saint's heart is the counterpane to God's law. The law is within his heart, (Psa. 40:8), and as it is in the Hebrew, in *the midst of his bowels.* God has infused a principle of grace into his inward parts, whereby he is not only inclined, but enabled to walk in all the commandments of the law blameless. A true saint hides the law in his heart, as a choice jewel in a most precious cabinet, as David says, (verse 9), "I have hid thy law in my heart;" hid it as a rare treasure. So does every saint, and therefore cannot but delight in it.

4. Because the same Holy Spirit that wrote the Word dwells in every true saint. It is certain that all

Scripture is of Divine inspiration, and that the "holy men of God spoke as they were guided by the Holy Ghost." And it is as certain that the same Holy Ghost dwells in every saint, (Rom. 8:11). And by virtue of the indwelling of the Spirit they are sweetly and powerfully drawn to make the law of God their chief delight.

5. Because it is God's indictment and invention. This reason is brought in the text, "Unless thy law," *etc.* It is the law of that God in whom they delight. It transcribes the mind and heart of God. A true saint sees the name, authority, power, wisdom, and goodness of God in every letter of it, and therefore cannot but take pleasure in it. It is an epistle sent down to him from the God of heaven. It is one of the greatest love-tokens that ever God gave to His Church. There are two great gifts that God has given to His people —the Word Christ, and the Word of Christ: both are unspeakably great; but the first will do us no good without the second.

6. A true saint cannot but delight in the Word of God, because it is his inheritance, (verse 111), "Thy testimonies have I taken as an heritage for ever, for they are the rejoicing of my heart." Therefore they were the rejoicing of his heart, because they were his everlasting inheritance.

7. Because he finds a sweetness in it. Delight is nothing else but a passion of the soul arising from the sweetness of the object that we enjoy. Things that are good, pleasant, suitable, and sweet, are the object of our delights; such is the Word of God to every true saint; it is "sweeter than the honey and the honey-comb," (Psa. 19:10); so also Psa. 119:103, "How sweet are thy words to my taste, yes, sweeter than honey to my mouth." A saint must needs delight in it, it is so suitable and so sweet.

8. Because he loves the law. Now that which we love we cannot but delight in, when we come to enjoy it A true saint does not only love the law, but he loves it

exceedingly: (Psa. 119:167), "My soul has kept thy testimonies, and I love them exceedingly." A true saint can say with David, (Psa. 119:97), "O how do I love thy law!" and verse 127, "I love thy commandments above gold, yes, above fine gold;" and verse 72, "The law of thy mouth is better to me than thousands of gold and silvers." Now because the saints of God are so enamored with the law of God, therefore it is that they cannot but delight in it, as David says, (Psa. 119:47), "I will delight myself in thy commandments, which I have loved." He that loves the commandments (as all saints do) cannot but delight in them.

Use. This shows that there are but few true saints amongst us. There are many bastard saints, and nominal saints, but few true and real saints. We live in an age wherein there were never more saints, and never fewer, never more by outward profession, and never fewer by a holy conversation. It is the property of a true saint to make the Word of God his darling and delights.

But where shall we find such saints? It is easy to find out men that can say, "gating and drinking is my delight, carding and dicing is my delight, reading of vain and trifling books is my delight, to satisfy the lust of the flesh is my delight." But where is the man that can truly say as David does—"The law of God is my delights, and the joy and rejoicing of my heart for ever?" Austin professes of himself, that before his conversion he took no pleasure in the Word of God. His proud heart, as he says, *would not stoop to the humble expressions of it.* After his conversion he was ravished with the beauty and excellency of the Scriptures; but before his conversion, he saw no excellency in them. Politian (though a great scholar, yet a notorious atheist) professes most blasphemously that he never lost more time than in reading the Scriptures. And it is reported of Plato, that when he had read the first chapter of Genesis,

he said, *This man says many things, but proveth nothing.* Where shall we find the man that puts a due estimation on the Word of God? that prizes it above gold, yes, above much find gold? "That rejoices in thy word, as much as in all riches," (verse 14); that can appeal to God, and say as David, (verse 159), "Consider, O Lord, how I love thy precepts;" and verse 97, "O how do I love thy law?" There are some men that can delight in anything but in God and His Word, and His ordinances. They can delight in the creatures of God, but cannot delight in the ordinances of God. They can delight in the gifts of God, in riches, and health, and honors; but they cannot delight in the God of these gifts. They can delight in books of philosophy and humanity, but they cannot delight in the Word of God.
Mark the sad condition that these are in.

It is a certain sign that there is a veil over their eyes and hearts, that they are not yet anointed with Christ's eye-salve, that the god of the world has blinded their eyes, that they cannot see the glorious excellences of the law of God.

It is certain that they are not born anew, for if they were new-born babes, they would desire the sincere milk of the Word.

It is certain that the law of God is not yet written in their hearts; and that the Spirit of God does not dwell in them. It is certain that they have no part nor portion in the Word of God, that they never tasted the sweetness that is in it, and that they have no true love to God, nor to His word. It is a true saying, *He that loves a king will love his law.* And I may say, *He that loves God will love the law of God,* which is nothing else but His image, and His picture, His last will and testament, His blessed love-token. And therefore, if you delight not in the law of God, it is evident you do not delight in the God of this law. And if you delight not in God, He will not delight in you; unless it be to "laugh at your destruction," as it is Prov. 1:26.

Question. But how shall I know whether that I do delight in the Word of God or not? *Answer.* You shall know it by these notes:—

1. He that delights in God's law will be very frequent in the meditating and reading of it, and very often in the speaking of it. So David says, (Psa. 1:2), "His delight is in the law of the Lord, and therein he will meditate day and night" And Psa. 119:97, "Oh how do I love thy law! it is my meditation all the day." So also verses 15, 16, 23. He that takes pleasure in the law, he will be often thinking of it; as Christ says, (Matt. 6:21), "Where the treasure is, there the heart will be also." If the Word of God is your treasure, you will meditate on it. You will frequently think of it; and when you begin to think of it, you will dwell on the thought of it, as a bee dwells, as it were, on the flower, to suck out the sweetness that is in it; and you will think of it with deep and serious meditations and contemplations; you will dive into the unsearchable riches and treasures that are in the Word. And as you will meditate on it, so you will be often and unwearisome in reading and perusing of it, and discoursing about it. A man that delights in hunting, is never weary of talking of hunting; and he that delights in the world, of speaking about the world; and if you delight in God's Word, you will be very frequent and never tire in discoursing of it.

2. If you delight in the Word of God, you will delight in the ministers and ambassadors of the Word, *lawfully commissioned* by Christ. For the great work of the ministry is to expound and apply the Word; and therefore if you disrespect the godly, learned, lawful ministry of the Word, you take no delight in the Word.

3. They that delight in the Word, will be at any cost to bring the Word to their congregations; they will

part with thousands of gold and silver, rather than with the Word. He that esteems the Word above thousands, will be willing to part with hundreds for the Word's sake. He will account a famine of the Word more bitter than a famine of bread; by how much the soul is better than the body, by so much will he be more troubled for a soul famine than a bodily.

4. He that delights truly in the law will sincerely labor to obey it, and be much grieved when it is disobeyed.

(1). He will sincerely labor to obey it; he will make the Word of God the man of his counsel, (verse 25). "Thy testimonies are my delight." But how does he prove that? In the following words, "and my counsellors." He will make the Word a "lamp to his feet, and a light to his paths," (verse 105). In all his undertakings he will inquire what God would have him to do, and he will make God's Word his compass to sail by; and pray with David, (verse 35), "Make me to go in the path of thy commandments, for therein do I delight."

(2). He will be much grieved when others transgress the law of God. David says, (verse 53), "Horror has taken hold on me, because of the wicked that forsake thy law." And verse 136, "Rivers of waters run down mine eyes because they keep not thy law."

And, therefore, you that delight in sin, you cannot be said to delight in the Word; and you that are not pained and grieved when others sin, you are not among the number of those that take pleasure in God's law, or in whom God takes pleasure.

Use 2. Let us make it appear that we are saints in deed and in truth, not only saints in man's, but in God's calendar, by following the example of holy David set down in the text. Let us make the law of God our joys and our delights. Let me speak to you in the words of the apostle, (Col. 3:16), "Let the word of God dwell richly in you," *etc.*, not only *with* you, but *in you.* And in the words of Christ, (John 5:39), "Search the Scriptures, for therein you hope to find eternal life." The Greek word signifies *to search,* as men do underground for *treasures,* or to search as men who dive under water for something that is *at the bottom.* Let us, with Job (23:12), esteem the Word of God "above our necessary food." Let us "love it above gold, yes, above fine gold;" let it be "dearer to us than thousands of gold and silver, sweeter than the honey and the honey-comb."

You that are gentlemen, remember what Jerome reports of Nepotianus, a young gentleman of Rome, who, by often and assiduous meditation of the Scriptures, made his breast the library of Christ. Remember what is said of King Alphonsus, that he read over the Bible fourteen times, together with such commentaries as those times afforded.

You that are scholars, remember Cranmer and Ridley; the former learned the New Testament by heart in his journey to Rome, the latter, in Pembroke-Hall walks, in Cambridge. Remember what is said of Thomas-a-Kempis, that he found rest nowhere, but in a corner with this book in his hand. And what is said of Beza, that when he was above fourscore years old, he could say perfectly by heart any Greek chapter in Paul's epistles.

You that are women, consider what Hierom says of Paula, Eustochiam, and other ladies, who were singularly versed in the Holy Scriptures.

Let all men consider that hyperbolical speech of Luther, that he would not live in Paradise without the Word; and with it, he could live well enough in hell. This speech of Luther's must be understood with a little allowance.

Question. May not a wicked man delight in the Word of God? Is it not said of Herod, (Mark 6:20), "That he heard John Baptist gladly?" and of the stony ground, (Luke 8:13), "That it received the word with joy?" Is it not said of the Israelites remaining wicked, that they delighted to know God's ways, and took delight in approaching to God? (Isa. 58:2). And of the Jews, (John 5:35), that they were willing for a season to rejoice in the light held forth by the preaching of John Baptist?

Answer. There is a wide and vast difference between the joy and delight which a true saint takes in God's Word, and that which may be found in a hypocrite.

1. The delight of a godly man is orderly and seasonable; it is the consequent of conviction and humiliation; for though joy be the great work of the Spirit, yet it is not the first work. First, the Spirit by the Word convinces and humbles, and then comforts; therefore Christ says, (Matt. 5:4), "Blessed are those that mourn, for they shall be comforted," and David says, (Psa. 126:5), "They that sow in tears shall reap in joy." But the joy of a hypocrite is unseasonable and disorderly; it is the first work. It is said of the stony ground, that when "they heard the word, they received it immediately with gladness," (Mark 4:16). It is not said they received it first with sorrow, and then with gladness. Here is mention of joy without any antecedent humiliation. No, the text says expressly, (Luke 8:6), "It lacked moisture," and therefore it withered away. There are many professors in our days that skip from sin to joy at first, that all in an instant are in the highest form of sin, and in the highest form of comfort; that skip out of the lap of the devil into the lap of joy. These are as a stony ground. These are wanton Christians; they sow before they plow; they do not know the bitterness of sin, and therefore in time of temptation fall away.

2. The delight that a godly man takes in the Word is a well-rooted delight. It is rooted in a humble,

good, and honest heart; as it is said of the good ground, (Luke 8:15). But the delight of a hypocrite is shallow and superficial; as his graces are slight and formal, so are his delights. Therefore it is said of the seed that fell on the stony ground, that it had "no root," (Luke 8:13; Matt. 13:5), "It wanted depth of earth;" and therefore when the sun arose it was scorched. The apostle hints, (Heb. 6:4), "And have tasted the good word of God." The delight of a wicked man in the Word is but a tasting and sipping, not soaking; a floating aloft in the river of Christ's blood, not diving down to the bottom. A man may taste a thing, and not like it—taste, and like it, and yet not come up to the price of it, as the young man in Matt. 19:22. He was very desirous to enjoy eternal life, but he would not part with his possessions for the obtaining of it. A cook tastes of the meat he dresses, but they only that are invited eat of it.

Tasting does not imply habitual grace. A man may taste that which he never digests nor concocts.

The Israelites tasted of the first fruits of the land of Canaan, and yet did not enter into Canaan. Such is the joy of the hypocrite. It is outward and superficial; but the delight of a true saint is inward, solid, and substantial. Jeremiah says, that the Word of God was the joy and rejoicing of his heart, and that he did eat it, (Jer. 15:16). He did not only taste it, but eat it. And Paul says, (Rom. 7:22), "I delight in the law of God after the inner man." His delights had depth of earth, they were well digested and concocted.

3. It is superlative and overtopping. A godly man delights more in God and His Word than in any worldly thing whatsoever. "Lord, lift thou up," says David, (Psa. 4:6-7), "the light of thy countenance on us: you have put gladness in my heart, more than in the time that their corn and their wine increased." So also Psa. 43:4, "To God my exceeding joy;" Psa. 137:6, "If I prefer not

Jerusalem above my chief joy." And Psa. 119:72, and verse 127. The delight of a saint in God's Word overtops all his creature delights and enjoyments, and for the joy he finds in it he will sell all that he has to purchase it, (Matt 13:44). But the joy of a wicked man is of an inferior nature, he rejoices more in corn, wine, and oil, *etc.* And when it comes into competition, he will leave his spiritual and heavenly rather than lose his creature and carnal pleasures. So Herod rejoiced in the word that John Baptist preached, but he rejoiced more in his Herodias; and when it came to the trial, he chose to behead John Baptist rather than to part with Herodias.

The stony ground, when persecution arose, parted with all its joy and faith, rather than it would lose its estate or life. As a godly man "rejoices in worldly things as though he rejoices not," (1 Cor. 7:30), so a wicked man rejoices in spiritual things as though he rejoiced not. In the old law those fowls that did both fly and swim were unclean. A wicked man would many times fly aloft in spiritual delights; but he would also bathe himself and swim in carnal pleasures; and his heart is more affected with worldly advancement and bodily recreations than with heavenly; and this is a sign that he is an unclean Christian; and that his delights in God and His Word are not right, because they are not overtopping and superlative.

4. It is powerful and soul-strengthening, full of life, vigor, and activity; it will enable the soul to do and suffer anything for God; it turns a prison into a paradise; it makes martyrdom to be as a bed of roses; it is armor of proof to steel us, and make us fit to endure afflictions, both for God and from God; therefore David says in the text, "Unless thy law had been my delights, I should then have perished in mine affliction." His delight in the law supported him from sinking. It is like oil to the wheels, like sails to the ship, and wings to the bird; but the

delight that a wicked man has in the Word is a powerless, dead, fruitless, and strengthless delight; it is as a paper helmet and a painted fire; it will not support him in the hour of adversity. The persons represented by the stony ground fell away, notwithstanding their joy, as soon as ever persecution arose for the gospel. But the joy of a true saint is soul-supporting and soul-upholding. The joy of the Lord is their strength, (Neh. 8:10).

5. The delight that a godly man has in the Word is sin excluding; it cannot consist with a delight in any sin; therefore David says, "Thy word have I hid in my heart, that I might not sin against thee," (Psa. 119:11). Sin is as a wooden window, to shut out the true joys of the Spirit. But now a wicked man, though he may delight in the Word, yet he also delights in sinning against the Word. Although Herod heard John Baptist gladly, yet he kept his Herodias; and though the Israelites delighted to know God's ways, yet they did not delight to walk in His ways. They were as a nation that did righteousness; he does not say they were such, but as a nation that did righteousness. And though they delighted to approach to God, yet they did not delight to obey that God before whom they approached; they took pleasure in sinning against God, as well as in serving of God, (Isa. 58). It was not a sin-excluding joy, and, therefore, it was false and counterfeit.

6. It is grace-increasing. The more a saint delights in the Word of God, the more careful he will be to obey the will of God, and to grow and increase in the grace of God; therefore David says, "My soul hath kept thy testimonies, for I love them exceedingly," (Psa. 119:167). And "I delight to do thy will, O my God; yes, thy law is within my heart," (Psa. 40:8). Because the law was written in his heart, therefore he delighted to do it. He that delights to keep God's law, God will give him more grace to keep it, according to that remarkable text, "I

have remembered thy name, O Lord, and have kept thy law: this I had, because I have kept thy precepts," (Psa. 119:55-56). What had David for keeping God's precepts? He had power to keep His law; that is, to grow and increase in keeping of it. As the prophet speaks of the knowledge of God, "Then shall we know, if we follow on to know the Lord," (Hos. 6:3), that is, if we industriously labor to know God, we shall have this reward, to be made able to know Him more. So may I say of the grace of God: he that delights to keep God's law shall have this reward, to be enabled to keep it more perfectly.

A true delight in God's Word is grace increasing. Grace is the mother of all true joy, (Isa. 32:17); and joy is as the daughter, and the mother and daughter live and die together. True spiritual delight ebbs and flows as grace ebbs and flows. As the wood is to the fire, oil to the flame, the shadow to the body, so is joy to grace. But now a wicked man, though he may have a kind of delight in God's Word, yet it is not a delight of the right kind, it does not argue that he has true grace in him.

A hypocrite is all joy and no grace. A giant in joy, and not so much as a dwarf in grace; like a green bough tied to a dead tree. He is in the highest form of joy, and not so much as in the lowest form of grace.

7. The delight that a godly man has in the Word, is not only a delight in spiritual things, but a spiritual delight, grounded on spiritual aims and reasons. But the delight of a wicked man, though it be in spiritual things, yet it is but a natural delight. As a godly man spiritualizes carnal things, so an ungodly man callouses spiritual things. Austin before his conversion rejoiced much to hear Ambrose preach, but it was because of his eloquence, as he says, not on a spiritual account. A wicked man may follow a preacher, and delight in his preaching, because of his elegant words and rhetorical expressions—because "he is to him as a very lovely song

of one that has a pleasant voice," etc., as it is said in Ezek. 32:32. Or out of novelty, because newly come, as the Israelites delighted in manna at first, but afterwards loathed it; or because he loves his person; or out of a desire to obtain a form of knowledge in heavenly things. The Pharisees delighted to do many spiritual things out of vainglory, Jehu delighted to do the will of God, but it was for his own ends. Stella is of opinion that the devil persuaded Herod to hear John Baptist gladly; and to reverence him, and to do many things, that so he might hold him the faster in his possession. The devil had him sure by one sin, and therefore he provoked him to do some good things, that so he might rock him asleep in presumption, and by his good things he might quiet his conscience, and put a fair gloss on his incestuous practices. A man may rejoice in spiritual things on sinful grounds and reasons. But now a true saint delights in the Word on a spiritual account, because it is God's Word, and God would have him delight in it; because it is his guide to glory, the way by which he is sanctified. It is both a cistern to contain the glorious mysteries of salvation, and a conduit to convey God and grace into his soul.

In a word, he delights in it because it is holy and pure; he can say with David, "Thy word is very pure, therefore thy servant loves it," (Psa. 119:140). This no wicked man can truly say.

8. The delight that a godly man takes in the Word is without any reservation or distinction. He delights in the whole Word of God—in the commanding and threatening word, as well as in the promising word; he beholds God and His wisdom and goodness in every verse, and therefore he can say with Hezekiah, "Good is the word of the Lord," (Psa. 39:8). He has the whole law written in his heart, and rejoices in every tittle of it. But a wicked man has his reservations

and distinctions; he may delight in the promising word, but he undervalues the commanding word, and turns a deaf ear to the threatening word. It is said of the Jews, that they rejoiced in the light of John Baptist; but it is not said, they rejoiced in his heat He was a burning and a shining light; they rejoiced in his shining, but not in his burning. It is hardly possible for a wicked man remaining wicked, to rejoice in the burning zeal, holiness, and strictness of a John Baptist But a godly man delights both in the light and heat of the Word.

9. It is an abiding delight;" Everlasting consolation," (2 Thess. 2:16); "Your joy no man taketh from you," (John 16:22). It is as a fixed star. But the delight of a wicked man in the Word is as the crackling of thorns on the fire, and as the corn that grew on the stony ground, which quickly sprung up, and as quickly withered, (Luke 8:6). Therefore it is said of the Jews, "they rejoiced in his light for a season," (John 5:3). A wicked man's delight in the Word is but as a blazing star, which is quickly extinguished. He may rejoice in the Word while he is hearing of it, but it quickly vanishes away. He is like to a man that comes into a pleasant garden, and is delighted with the smell of it while he is there. But a child of God makes a posy of these flowers, to refresh him when he is out. He delights to read and to keep the law of God continually, for ever and ever, (Psa. 119:45).

Let us, I beseech you, labor with all labor for this superlative, well-rooted, powerful, spiritual, sin-excluding, grace-increasing, and abiding delight in the whole Word of God.

Ques. What must we do, that we may be enabled so to make the law of God our delights?

Answer. 1. You must seriously study the excellency of God's Word; this made David prize it so much, and love it so much, (Psa. 19:7-11). The Word of

God has God for its Author; and therefore must needs be full of infinite wisdom and eloquence, even the wisdom and eloquence of God. There is not a word in it but breathes out God, and is breathed out by God. It is an invariable rule of faith, and unerring and infallible guide to heaven. It contains glorious revelations and discoveries nowhere else to be found. It has a manifesting, convincing, soul-humbling, soul-directing, soul-converting, and soul-comforting power and efficacy in it, as appears by these scriptures—Heb. 4:12; 1 Cor. 14:24, 25; 1 Kings 21:29; Psa. 119:105; 2 Cor. 3:16; Psa. 119:50. And therefore to delight in the Word, and the God that made it, is not only our duty, (Psa. 37:4), but it is recorded in Scripture as our privilege, and as the great reward that God would bestow on those that keep holy the Sabbath day. "Then thou shalt delight thyself in the Lord," (Isa. 58:13-14). This shall be your great reward.

2. You must fixedly ponder the necessity of practicing this duty; for if you delight in God's law, God will delight in you. If the law be your beloved, you are God's beloved; if you take no pleasure in his Word, his soul will take no pleasure in you.

3. You must pray for the grace of illumination. Whensoever you take the Bible in your hand to read in it, pray David's prayer, "Open thou mine eyes, that I may behold wondrous things out of thy law," (Psa. 119:18). Philosophers observe that light is the chariot of influence: as it begets the flower in the field, the gold in the mineral; so the foundation of all regeneration is illumination. Pray that God would open your eyes that you may understand the Scriptures, as He did to His apostles, (Luke 24:45); that He would take away the veil that is on your hearts.

4. Pray that He that made you creatures would make you new creatures, that as new-born babes you

may desire the sincere milk of the Word.

5. Pray that God would fulfill that excellent promise in Jer. 31:33: that He would put His law in your inward parts, and write it in your hearts, and then you cannot but heartily delight in it.

6. Pray to God to give you the same Spirit that wrote the Word, to enable you to delight in it.

7. Pray for a spiritual palate, that you may not only delight in spiritual things, but have a spiritual delight in spiritual things. It is said of the lioness, that when she has once tasted of the sweetness of man's flesh, she is never satisfied until she has more of it. He that has tasted of the good Word of God, and not only tasted, but eaten it, and digested it into good nourishment, he will not only delight in it, but he will delight in it above gold, yes, above fine gold, and he will never be satisfied until he be filled with the fullness of that God that made it.

SERMON 3

Psa. 119:92, "Unless thy law had been my delights, I should then have perished in mine affliction."

Now I come to speak of the proposition that is clearly held forth in the *text,*

Doctrine 3. *That the Word of God delighted in is the afflicted saint's antidote against ruin and destruction:* "Unless thy law had been my delights, I should," *etc.* The Word of God is the sick saint's salve, the dying saint's cordial, a most precious medicine to keep God's people from perishing in time of affliction. This upheld Jacob from sinking when his brother Esau came furiously marching to destroy him, (Gen. 21:12), "And thou saidst, I will surely do thee good," *etc.* The promise of God supported him. This also upheld Joshua, and enabled him courageously to fight the Lord's battles because God had said He would never leave him nor forsake him, (Josh. 1:5). Melancthon says that the Landgrave of Hesse told him at Dresden, that it had been impossible for him to have borne up under the manifold miseries of so long an imprisonment but for the comforts of the Scriptures in his heart.

There are eight things may be said, among many other, in commendation of the Word of God:—

1. It is the magazine and storehouse of all comfort and consolation. There is no condition but one that a man can be in, but he may find soul-supporting comfort for it out of the Word. Indeed, if you resolve to go on in sin, the Word cannot comfort thee; it threatens hell and damnation to all such. If the God of heaven can make such miserable, they shall be miserable; but excepting this one, there is no condition so miserable but a man may fetch a cordial out of the Word to support him under it. Are you as empty of riches, and as full of

diseases, as Job under the Old Testament, and Lazarus under the New Testament? Are your sins, with which you are willing to part, many and great? Is your conscience exceedingly wounded and disquieted? Does the devil roar on you with hideous temptations? Let your condition be never so sad, the Word of God is able to afford you comfort under it; for it is the Word of that God who is the God of all consolation. There is no kind of true comfort, but here it is to be had,—here are cordials of all sorts: comforts under bodily troubles, and comforts under soul troubles. There is no monarch can furnish his table with such variety of delicacies as God has furnished His Word with variety of comforts.

2. The Word of God is not only the magazine of all true comfort, but the fountain from where it is derived. All the comfort that you receive by reading of good books is fetched out of this book. All the refreshings that the ambassadors of Christ administer to you are borrowed from this fountain. As the king of Israel answered the woman that cried out, saying, "Help, my lord, O king," (2 Kings 6:26-27), "If the Lord do not help thee, whence shall I help thee?" will all the true ministers of Christ say to any distressed soul that cries out for comfort: How can *we* comfort you if the *Word of God* does not comfort you? All our comforts must be fetched from there.

3. It will comfort us at such a time when no outward thing can comfort us; and that is when we are under soul-agonies, and when our soul sits on our lips ready to depart; when we are falling into the ocean of eternity, then, even then, the promises of the Word will comfort us, when gold and silver, father and mother, friends and physicians, are *miserable* comforters,—then will one promise out of the Word fill us full of joy unspeakable and glorious.

4. The comforts of the Word exceed all other

comforts, for they are pure and purifying, sure and satisfying; they are soul-supporting, soul-comforting, and soul-ravishing—they are durable and everlasting. The comforts of the world are not worthy to be named that day in which we speak of the comforts of the Word. At best they are but bodily, unsatisfying, and transitory; many times they are sinful and soul-damning.

5. The Word of God is not only a magazine and a fountain of comfort, but also a touchstone by which we must try all our comforts whether they are true and real or no. All joys, hopes, and assurances must be tried by the Word, and if not rightly grounded.

6. It is an apothecary's shop, or a physician's dispensatory, out of which we may fetch all manner of medicines to cure all the diseases of our souls. Are you spiritually lame, blind, or dumb? *etc.* The Word will open blind eyes, make the dumb to speak, and the lame to walk. If dead in sins and trespasses, the Word, when it is the sword of the Spirit, will quicken you: it is as a corrosive to eat sin out of your heart; therefore David says, "I have hid thy word in mine heart, that I might not sin against thee."

7. It is a spiritual armory, out of which we may fetch all manner of weapons to conquer the devil and his temptations, (2 Cor. 10:4). It is that little brook out of which every David may fetch five smooth stones to destroy the devil. These five smooth stones are five texts of Scripture—three of these Christ took out of the brook of the Word, by which he subdued the devil, (Matt. 4:4, 7, 10).

8. It is the sun of the Christian world. As the sun is the light of the natural world, and without it the world is but a chaos and a dungeon full of darkness; so is the Word of God the light of the spiritual world, without which a Christian is under an eternal night. Therefore David says, "Thy word is a lamp to my feet, and a light to

my path," (Psa. 119:105). What would all the world avail if there were no sun to enlighten it? And what comfort would all the wealth of it afford us if there were no Word to instruct and counsel us? For this is the Christian's compass to sail to heaven by, his staff to walk withal to heaven, his spiritual floats to keep his soul from drowning, the cork to keep up the net of his soul from sinking. Afflictions are like the lead of the net which weighs it down; but the Word is as the cork which keeps it up, that it does not sink. So says David in the text, "Unless thy law had been my delights," *etc.*

Use 1. If the Word of God be of such invaluable excellency, absolute necessity, and of such admirable *use*,

1. Let us bless God exceedingly for revealing His will to us in the Word. It was a great honor and privilege to the Jews that to them "were committed the oracles of God," (Rom. 3:2). And it is our great happiness that we have not only the same oracles of God which they have, but an addition of the New Testament for the clearer discovery of the mysteries of salvation to us. If God be to be praised for every crumb of bread we eat, much more for giving us His Word, which is the bread of life, and the only food of our souls. Blessed be God, who has not only given us the book of the creatures and the book of nature to know Himself and His will by, but also, and especially, the book of the Scriptures, whereby we come to know those things of God and of Christ which neither the book of nature nor of the creatures can reveal to us.

Let us bless God, not only for revealing His will in His Word, but for revealing it by writing. Before the time of Moses, God discovered His will by immediate revelations from heaven, "But we have a surer word of prophecy," (2 Pet. 1:19),—surer to us than a voice from heaven; for the devil says the apostle, "transforms himself into an angel of light." He has his apparitions and revelations; he is God's ape, and, in imitation of God, he appears to his disciples, and makes them believe that it is God that appears, and not the devil. So, he appeared to Saul in the likeness of Samuel. And if God should now at this day discover His way of worship, and His Divine will by revelations, how easily would men be deceived, and mistake diabolical delusions for Divine revelations; and therefore let us bless God for the written Word, which is surer and safer, as to us, than an immediate revelation. There are some that are apt to think, that if an angel should come from heaven and reveal God's will to them, it would work more on them than the written Word; but I would have these men study the conference between Abraham and Dives, (Luke 16:27-31), "They have Moses and the prophets," if they will not profit by them, neither would they profit by any that should come out of hell, or down from heaven to them; for it is the same God that speaks by His written Word, and by a voice from heaven. The difference is only in the outward clothing; and therefore if God's speaking by writing will not amend us, no more will God's speaking by a voice. Oh, bless God exceedingly for the written Word! Let us cleave close to it, and not expect any revelations from heaven of new truths, but say with the apostle, as in Gal. 1:8-9.

Use 2. Let us prize the Word of God above gold, yes, above fine gold. Let us read it diligently, reverently, praying to God to give us the same Spirit that wrote it to enable us to understand it, and conscientiously to practice it. Let us make it the joy and rejoicing of our heart; and, as it is in the text, let us make it our delights; but of this I speak in the former point. The only motive I shall now use to persuade you to make the Word your delights shall be this in the text, because it will keep you from perishing in the time of your greatest affliction; it will comfort you when you have most need of it—that is, under heart-sinking afflictions, and at the hour of death; and it will comfort you when all outward comforts and creatures fail. It will be food to strengthen your weak faith—medicine to cure the remainder of corruption; it will be a cordial to revive your drooping spirits and fainting souls; it will make you more than conquerors over all temptations and distresses.

But now the great question is how a child of God ought to manage and make use of the Word of God, so as to make it a conduit of support and comfort in the day of his greatest afflictions.

Answer. To be able to do this, there is a great deal of spiritual wisdom and understanding required; for the Word to many people is like Saul's armor to David, which was so cumbersome to him that he could not wear it.

There are many know not how to use the Word so as to be comforted by it. As the woman of Samaria told Christ, (John 4:11), "The well is deep, and you have nothing to draw with;" so may I say, *The Word of God is a deep well, it is a well of salvation, but it is deep, and the deeper the sweeter,* but most people want buckets to draw with—they want a spiritual art (Isa. 4) to fetch out of these wells of salvation *divine* support and consolation; and therefore to help you in this great work you must know—

The Word of That the Word of God may be divided into three parts into *commandments, threatenings,* and *promises.* And though a Christian must not neglect the commanding and threatening word; yet, if ever he would make the Word a channel of Divine comfort, he must study the promising Word; for the promises are a Christian's *magna charta* for heaven. All comfort must be built on a Scripture promise, else it is presumption, not true comfort. The promises are the food of faith, and the soul of faith. As faith is the life of a

Christian, so the promises are the life of faith: faith is a dead faith, if it has no promise to quicken it As the promises are of no use without faith to apply them, so faith is of no use without a promise to lay hold on. And the great reason why the people of God walk uncomfortably in their afflictions is because they do not chew the promises. They are rare cordials; but as a man cannot taste the sweetness of a cordial unless he chew it, no more can we receive any spiritual refreshment from the promises unless we meditate on them. The promises are as a mine full of rich treasure; but, as mines, unless we dig deep into them, we can never get the gold and silver hid in them, no more can we enjoy the soul-ravishing comfort of the promises, unless we dig into them by a serious consideration of them. They are as a garden full of rare flowers, able to sweeten any condition. But because we do not walk in this garden, and pick-out these flowers, hence it is that we live so disconsolately and dejectedly under our afflictions. There are many rare stories declaring the comfort that some of God's saints have received from the promises in the day of their distress. Mr. Bilney, that blessed martyr, was much wounded in conscience by reason of the great sin he committed in subscribing to Popish errors; but he was much comforted by reading those words, (1 Tim. 1:15), "This is a faithful saying, and worthy of all acceptation, that Jesus Christ came into the world to save sinners, of which I am the chief." Beza was supported under his troubles by the words of Christ in John 10:27-29. Mr. Bolton tells us of one that was upheld under great affliction, and comforted from Isa. 26:3; of another from Isa. 57:15. I knew a young maid that went triumphantly to heaven by the refreshing she found in that well-known text, Matt 11:28, and many that have been wonderfully cheered by reading the 8th of the Romans, and by that text, (1 John 3:14), "We know that we have passed from death to life, because we love the brethren." The truth is, there is no promise but, if God be pleased to enlighten it, and show us our interest in it, will afford a harvest of joy. It is with promises as it is with sermons—that once heard, it may not at all work on us, but the same sermon at another time may exceedingly affect us. And the same text of Scripture which sometimes does not at all comfort us, may at another time convey much comfort to us. Two men troubled in conscience may both of them read the same chapter and heard the same sermon, and one of them may have his troubled mind pacified, and the other continue troubled; and the reason is, because the Spirit of God makes the Word effectual to one, and not to the other. How often has a distressed saint read Matt. 11:28; 1 Tim. 1:15; John 10:27-28; Isa. 26:3; 57:15; 1 John 3:14, and found no comfort in reading of them? But if the Spirit of God comes in and opens his eyes to behold the rich mercies wrapped up in these promises, and his interest in them, they would fill him with comfort above expression. And therefore if ever you would make the Word of God God's instrument to convey support and comfort to you in the time of soul-sinking afflictions, you must study the promises, and pray to God that His Spirit may irradiate them, and show you the fullness of them, and your interest in them.

Question. How must we improve the promises, so as to make them spiritual bladders, to keep us from being drowned in the deep waters of affliction?

Answer. You must do three *things:*

I. You must make a catalogue of the promises.

II. You must seriously ponder and meditate on them.

III. You must apply them to your own souls as belonging to you in particular.

I. You must make a catalogue of the promises;

you must gather them up, as they lie scattered in the Word, into a spiritual journal and bind them together. You must do as they that gather up ends of gold and silver; you must lose none. Every promise is as a ray of gold; as a star in the firmament. And though there are stars of divers magnitudes, differing from one another in glory, yet every star has its beauty and benefit; so, though some promises are more glorious than others, (like the sun in comparison of the moon), yet every promise has its beauty and luster; and as starlight in a dark night is very comfortable, so in the dark night of affliction every little promise will afford unspeakable comfort to a troubled soul.

To help you in making this catalogue, give me leave to suggest three things:

1. Be sure to make it in time of health. Woe be to those that have their promises to gather when they should make use of them. You that slight the promises in prosperity, shall receive no comfort from them in adversity.

2. Do not forget to treasure up all those promises which God has made to His children in the day of their adversity. As, for example, God has promised in all our afflictions to be with us, (Isa. 43:2), "When thou passest through the waters, I will be with thee, and through the rivers, they shall not overflow thee," *etc.* He will be with you, to protect and direct you, to support and comfort you. If three saints be put into the fiery furnace, the Son of God will make the fourth, (Dan. 3:25).

(1). God will be afflicted in all our afflictions, (Isa. 63:9). He suffers in all our sufferings, (Acts 9:4).

(2). He will make our beds in our sickness, (Psa. 41:2). He will condescend to the lowest office for our ease and refreshment.

(3). He will know our souls in adversity, (Psa. 31:7). He will know us, to pity us, and to succor, and to help us.

(4). He will keep us from the evil of all afflictions, (Job 5:19). God has not promised to keep His people from afflictions, but to keep them from the hurt of them. Though they are not good in themselves, yet he will turn them to our good, (Heb. 12:10; 1 Cor. 11:32; Jer. 24:5). The good figs were carried into captivity for their good. God has promised that all "things shall work together for our good," (Rom. 8:28); not only all ordinances, *etc.*, but all afflictions, *etc.*

(5). God has promised to lay no more on us than we are able to bear, but either to give us less pain or greater patience, (1 Cor. 10:13). And though in a little wrath He hid His face from us for a moment, yet with everlasting kindness will He have mercy on us, *etc.* (Isa. 54:7, 8). These, and many such-like promises, will be as so many spiritual cordials to revive our fainting spirits, and as so many pillars to uphold us under the greatest affliction.

3. For the completing of this catalogue, you may make use of many excellent books written for this purpose, wherein you shall have promises of all kinds, both spiritual and temporal, gathered together. Yet let me advise you not to rest satisfied with the collections of others, but when you read the Bible, and meet with a suitable promise with which God is pleased to affect your hearts, take the pains to write it down, and one such promise of your own writing will work more powerfully on your souls than many others of another's gathering. So much for the first— make a catalogue of the promises.

TO THE READER

Reader, this and the following sermon contains a large discourse about the promises, which because it may be thought by some to be impertinent to the text, and rather a digression from it, than an explication of it, I crave leave to inform you of two things.

1. That the promises are the principal ground of comfort to a child of God in the day of his adversity. They are his chief city of refuge when all creature-comforts fail; when he suffers shipwreck of all human props, these are his planks on which he swims safe to the shore of heaven. All comfort that is not founded on a promise is delusion, not true consolation. And therefore a discourse about them cannot rationally be interpreted as inapplicable to the text.

2. That there are divers particulars added to the sermons concerning the nature, necessity, excellency, and usefulness of the promises, which were not mentioned in the preaching of them. And if any of them shall appear to be heterogenial to the text, yet if they prove serviceable to heighten the esteem of the promises, and to quicken you to a more serious and frequent meditation on them, and application of them, I hope you art not at all injured; and I may justly desire that you would not be offended.

It is reported of St. Austin, in his life written by Possidius, that by a digression in one of his sermons from his text, he converted a heretic from his erroneous opinion. If any passage in these two sermons prove useful to turn you from your sinful negligence, and to awaken you to a more diligent study of the precious promises, I shall account it a happy and blessed digression. For herein especially consists the difference between a religious Christian and a moral man: a moral man will abstain from the outward acts of sin; but he does not know what it is to live on promises; he never tasted any sweetness in a promise; he lives on creatures, not on promises; and therefore when creatures fail, his heart sinks like a stone, and he is at his wits' end and faith's end. But a religious Christian lives on promises, and not on creatures; and therefore when creatures fail, he has the promises to live on; he labors to taste the sweetness that is in them. He lives on promises, when providence seems to run cross to promises. They are his fiery chariot, to carry him up to heaven. If, then, these ensuing sermons inflame your affections with a greater love to the promises, and a greater care to meditate on them, and to get an interest in them, you have cause to bless God, and to pray *for*

Thy unworthy servant in Christ,

EDM. CALAMY.

SERMON 4

Psa. 119:92, "Unless thy law had been my delights, I should then have perished in mine affliction."

He that would improve the promises, so as to make them spiritual bladders to keep him from being drowned in the deep waters of affliction, must not only make a catalogue of the promises, but he must *also*—

II. Fixedly and seriously meditate on them; first, he must treasure up these jewels in his heart, and then unlock them by meditation; first, he must make his journal, and then drink from it. The Word of God, as I have said, is a garden full of excellent promises, as so many choice flowers; and it is our duty to walk often in this garden, to gather up all the flowers that lie scattered in it into several nosegays, to bind them together, if I may so speak, with the thread of faith, and then every day to smell of them. The promises are the saints' legacies left them by Christ in His last will and testament. The saints are called the "heirs of the promises," (Heb. 6:17). And if they would be filled full of joy in the day of their distress, they must be frequent in reading these legacies. The promises are, as it were, the breasts of God, full of the milk of grace and comfort; and it is our duty to be sucking out, by meditation, the milk of grace and comfort contained in them. That which the prophet says of the Church of Christ may as truly be said of the promises of Christ, "Rejoice, O ye people of God, and be glad, all ye that have an interest in the promises: rejoice for joy, all ye that are mourners in Sion, that ye may suck and be satisfied with the breath of their consolations, that you may milk out, and be delighted with the abundance of joy and comfort contained in them." The promises are the saints' cordials, the saints' planks to swim to heaven on, the saints' fiery chariot to carry them up to heaven. And the great reason why they walk so uncomfortably, so disconsolately, and so unbelievingly, in the time of their tribulation, is because they do not smell of these sweet fragrances, they do not chew these cordials, they do not read over these spiritual legacies, they do not, by serious meditation and consideration, suck out the comfort comprehended in them. For as fire will not warm us unless we tarry at it, and as a bee cannot suck out the honey that is in a flower unless she abide on it, no more can a child of God receive support and consolation from the promises in the hour of temptation, unless he seriously and solemnly ponder and meditate on them.

There is a double difference between a presumptuous sinner, and a poor, humble, distressed child of God.

1. A presumptuous sinner studies nothing but the promising word: He slights the commanding, and the threatening Word. The Word commands him to keep holy the Sabbath day, not to love the world nor to lust, but he turns a deaf ear to it. The Word threatens to wound the hairy scalp of every one that goes on in his wickedness; but because God is patient and long-suffering, therefore he does not regard it. But as for the promising Word, he snatches at it, he does not truly lay hold on it, but snatches at it, before it belongs to him, and spider-like, sucks the poison of sin out of it, and makes of it a cradle to rock himself asleep in sinful courses. Because God has promised, that whensoever a sinner turns from his sins which he has committed, he shall surely live and not die, therefore he delays and postpones his turning from sin.

But now a poor, distressed, humble Christian fails on the contrary part; he pours on the commanding and threatening Word, but never ponders the promising Word. God, *he says*, commands me to love Him with all my heart and soul, to wash my heart from iniquity, to love my enemies, to cut off my right hand, and to pluck out my right eye, *etc.* But I cannot perform these commands; therefore surely I shall never be saved. God, *he says*, has threatened to curse every one that continues not in everything that is written in His law to do it, and therefore surely I am accursed. But he never studies nor ponders the promising Word, for if he did, he would quickly know three things for his everlasting comfort:

(1.) That there is nothing required by God in His Word as our duty, but on us as His gift, or the saints have prayed to God for it as His gift. God commands us to love Him, but He has promised to circumcise our hearts to love Him, *etc.*, (Deut. 30:6; Ezek. 18:31; 36:26; Jer. 32:40; Micah 7:19; Rom. 6:14). God commands us to fear Him, to turn ourselves from our transgressions, and to make ourselves a new heart and a new spirit.

But He has promised to give us a new heart and a new spirit; to put His fear in our hearts that we shall never depart from Him; and to turn us from our evil ways. The saints of God also have prayed to God for this, as the fruit of His free mercy, (Jer. 31:18; Lam. 5: 21). There is nothing commanded in the covenant of works but God has promised it in the covenant of grace, (Isa. 26:12; Jer. 31:33); in some measure to work it in us; for He has promised to work all our works in us, and to write His law (not one commandment of it only, but the whole law) in our hearts, and to put it in our inward parts, and to cause us to walk in His ways.

(2.) That God under the covenant of grace, will for Christ's sake accept of less than He requires in the covenant of works. He requires perfection of degrees, but He will accept of perfection of parts; He requires us to live without sin, but He will accept of our sincere endeavors to do it. "If there be a willing mind, it is accepted according to that a man has, and not according to that he has not," (2 Cor. 8:12).

(3). That though he cannot in his own person perform all that God commands, yet Jesus Christ, as his surety, and in his stead, has fulfilled the law for him, and that God will accept of Christ's perfect, as a cover for his imperfect, righteousness. That Christ has redeemed him from the curse of the law, being made a curse for him. That the threatenings of the law are serpents without a sting, and that Christ has taken away the power and force of them.

Did a broken-hearted and wounded sinner ponder and meditate on these things, they would fill him full of joy and comfort; he would fly from the covenant of works to the covenant of grace; from his own unrighteousness to the righteousness of Christ; and from the commanding and threatening Word to the promising Word; he would say, Lord, You command me to walk in Your statutes, and to keep Your laws; this I cannot do of myself, but You have promised to cause me to walk in Your ways, and to write Your law in my heart. Lord, give me power to do what You command, and then command what You will.

2. A presumptuous sinner is always studying the promising Word, to bolster up himself in sin, but he never studies his sins and iniquities, to repent for them, and from them. He meditates on the promises to harden his heart in sin, but not at all on his sins to humble himself for them, and to turn from them.

But now, on the contrary, a poor distressed Christian pores on his iniquities and corruptions, but never minds himself of the promises; and this makes him live so dejectedly and disconsolately. A wicked man studies his corruptions too little—a distressed Christian too much. If he did study the promises, as much as he does his corruptions, he would not walk so uncomfortably.

Wherefore if ever you would make the Word of God a conduit of comfort in the day of your distress, you must not only meditate on the commanding and threatening Word, but on the *promising Word*. The commandments and threatenings must drive you to the promises; you must not only study your corruptions to humble you, but also the promises to comfort you. I do not say you must not study your corruptions, but you must join the study of the promises together with them. If Abraham had minded only the deadness of Sarah's womb, and of his own body, he had never believed, *etc.*, but he was strong in faith, and did not stagger, because he considered not his own body now dead, when he was about an hundred years old, nor the deadness of Sarah's womb, but was fully persuaded, that what God had promised, He was able to perform, (Rom. 4:10, 20-21; Heb. 11:11). If Sarah had considered only that she was past age, she would never have believed that she should have a child; but she eyed the promise, and judged Him faithful who had promised, and that made her believe. If a saint of God looks only downwards on the deadness of his heart, and meditates only on his sins and infirmities, he will never be comforted in the day of his distress. But he must also look upwards to the promises, seriously ponder and fixedly study them; which will be as strong pillars to support him, and keep him from falling into despair, in the hour of tribulation.

Question. What are the meditations which we must have in reference and relation to the promises in the day of our distress?

Answer. I will rank them into nine particulars.

I. You must meditate on the three great truths already mentioned.

1. The first is that God commands nothing as our duty which He has not promised as His gift.

2. That God, in the covenant of grace, will accept

of less than He requires in the covenant of works.

3. That if we truly believe in Christ, God will accept of His righteousness as a satisfaction for our unrighteousness.

II. You must meditate on the excellency and preciousness or the promises; they are called exceeding: great and precious promises. They are precious in five respects:—

1. Because they cost a great price (even the blood of Christ) to purchase them. They are all made to us in Christ and for Christ; they are in Him *Yes*, and in Him *Amen*, (2 Cor. 1:20). The covenant (which is the cabinet of all the promises) was sealed with His blood.

2. Because they assure us of great and precious things; they assure us of our interest in God, of our justification, reconciliation, adoption, sanctification, and glorification; heaven itself is nothing else but the enjoyment of the promises, (Heb. 6:12). The promises are heaven folded up: heaven is the promise unfolded. For the promises are nothing else but the eternal purposes of God towards His children made manifest. The purposes of God are His concealed promises, and the promises are His revealed purposes. The promises are the kisses of Jesus Christ— they discover His dear love; and when He discovers to us our interest in them, then He kisses us with the kisses of His mouth, and fills us with joy unspeakable and glorious. They are made by God, and they make over God to us as our portion, and Christ as our Saviour, and the Spirit as our sanctifier, and all good things both here and hereafter as our inheritance, and therefore may well be called "exceeding great and precious promises."

3. Because they put a price on the New Testament; for wherein does the New Testament exceed the Old unless it be in this—because it is founded on better promises, (Heb. 8:6), and brings in a better hope,

(Heb. 7:19).

4. Because they put a price on all the blessings of God. A little mercy reached out to us as a fruit of a promise is more worth than a world of blessings coming to us merely by way of providence. A man may receive blessings from God on a double account, either by way of providence or by way of promise.

(1). By way of providence: So God gives the earth to the sons of men, (Psa. 115:16). So He gave one hundred twenty and seven provinces to Ahasuerus. So He sets up the basest of men to rule over nations, (Dan. 4:7).

(2). By way of promise. So, He gives health, wealth, and all outward comforts to His children. For "godliness has the promise of this life and that which is to come," (1 Tim. 4:8). Now, you must know that a little blessing coming to us as a fruit of the promise is more worth than a thousand blessings coming to us only by way of providence. And therefore David says, "A little that the righteous man has, is better than the riches of many wicked," (Psa. 37:16). And the reasons are,—

1st. Because blessings given by virtue of a promise are signs of God's special love, and come flowing to us from the same love with which God gives us Christ—they are the fruit of covenant love,

2d. Because we have them as blessings. A man may have a blessing, and yet not have it as a blessing. The Israelites had quails sent them immediately from God, which was a blessing in itself, but was not sent to them as a blessing; for while "the meat was in their mouths, the wrath of God came on them," (Psa. 17:7, 30-31). The wicked have blessings, but not as blessings, but as the cup in Benjamin's sack, which proved a snare to him rather than a mercy. But the godly have blessings as blessings: they have grace with them to improve them for God's glory; they have not only the blessings, but a thankful heart for them, and a fruitful heart under them, which is a certain sign that they have them as blessings.

3d. Because they are pledges to them of better mercies, and beginnings of better; they are not their wages, but an earnest of heaven. Now, a farthing given as an earnest of a thousand a year, is more worth than many pounds given as a reward. A wicked man has, outward blessings as his portion, his heaven, his all; but a godly man that has them by virtue of a promise, has them as a pledge of heaven, and as a beginning of eternal mercies.

5. The promises are precious, because they produce great and precious effects. They are not only excellent in themselves, but are also very powerful and operative on all believers. The promises, as one says, sealed by the blood of Christ, ratified by the oath of God, testified by the Spirit of truth, delivered by the hand of mercy, and received by the hand of faith, are operative words, and produce rare effects in the soul. They have, (1.) A sanctifying power. (2.) A comforting power.

(1). A soul-sanctifying power. Therefore they are said to make us "partakers of the divine nature," (2 Pet 1:4). I say, of the divine nature, not by the communication of the divine essence, but by participation of divine grace. Not in a familistical sense, as if we were Godded into God, and Christed into Christ, but in a spiritual sense; we are by the promises made partakers of the divine nature, that is, of the divine graces, by which we are made like to God in holiness. The apostle tells us that they have a power to "cleanse us from all filthiness, both of flesh and spirit, and to enable us to perfect holiness in His fear," (2 Cor. 7:1).

(2.) A comforting power. They are able to comfort us in the worst of days and dangers. Oh, how precious is a promise to a distressed Christian in the hour of extremity! The sun is not more comfortable to a man in a dark dungeon, or food to a man ready to starve, or water to a man ready to die for thirst. The promises of God are *always* precious, but never more precious than in times of misery and calamity; and therefore let us in such times especially meditate on the preciousness of them.

III. You must meditate on the freeness of the promises. The promises are the outward discoveries of God's eternal love to His people. Now, nothing moved God to enter into covenant with them, and to engage Himself to them by promise, and thereby to become their debtor, but His free love and mercy; and therefore they are said to be given us of God, "Whereby are given to us exceeding great and precious promises," (2 Pet 1:4). God promises in His Word, not only to love us, but to love us freely. "I will heal their backsliding, and love them freely," (Hos. 14:4). The reason why God makes us His people, is not from any worth in us, but only because it pleases Him so to do. The Lord will not forsake his people for his great name's sake; because it pleased the Lord to make you his people," (1 Sam. 12:22). The Lord Jesus Christ, who is the great and fundamental promise, the root of the other promises, is freely tendered in the gospel, and freely given. "God so loved the world, that he gave his only begotten Son," *etc.*, (John 3:16). "Whosoever will, let him take the water of life freely," (Rev. 22:17).

IV. The fourth meditation: Meditate on the stability of the promises. You must meditate on the firmness, faithfulness, unchangeableness, and immutability of the promises: they are the promises of that God who cannot deny Himself. "Heaven and earth shall pass away, but one jot or tittle of the Word shall not pass." There is no promise which God has made, though never so improbable and impossible to flesh and blood, but it shall come to pass in due time; whatsoever He has promised in His goodness, He will perform by

His power. "God is not a man that he should lie, neither the son of man that he should repent: has he said, and shall he not do it? or has he spoken, and shall he not make it good?" (Num. 23:19). God has promised that the same bodies that die shall rise again at the last day. This is incredible to natural reason. The Stoics and Epicures derided it when it was preached by Paul, (Acts 17:32). But has God said it, and shall He not do it? Is the Lord's hand shortened? Therefore Christ tells the Sadducees, "You err, not knowing the Scriptures, and the power of God," (Matt 22:37). God is omnipotent, and therefore able to do above what we can ask or think. God has promised at the resurrection to make our vile bodies like to the glorious body of Christ. This is impossible to natural reason, but mark what the apostle says, "Who shall change our vile bodies, and fashion them like to his glorious body, according to the working whereby he is able even to subdue all things to himself," (Phi. 3:21). God has promised that before the end of the world there shall be a national conversion of the Jews, that the kingdoms of the world shall become the kingdoms of our Lord and Saviour, and that Babylon shall fall (Rom. 11:25; Rev. 16:15; 18:2). These are the promises of God, who cannot lie. "Faithful is he who has said it, who also will do it," (1 Thess. 5:24). Though the things promised seem impossible to men, yet with God all things are possible (Matt. 19:26). Therefore the apostle proves the future conversion of the Jews, by an argument drawn from the power of God. "God is able to graft them in again," (Rom. 11:23). The like is brought to prove the ruin of Antichrist. "Her plagues shall come in one day, death and mourning and famine, and she shall be utterly burnt with fire, for strong is the Lord God, who judgeth her," (Rev. 18:8). The promises are a firm foundation to build our salvation on—an anchor both sure and steadfast. When David was taken by the Philistines, he was so supported by the promise of God that he did not fear what man could do against him; therefore he repeats it three times, "In God I will praise his word, in God I will praise his word, in God I will praise his word," (that is, his word of promise), "I will not fear what flesh can do to me," (Psa. 56:3, 10). The Scripture builds all the hope and comfort of a Christian on the faithfulness of God. "God is faithful, who will not suffer you to be tempted above that you are able," *etc.*, (1 Cor. 10:13); "The Lord is faithful, who shall establish you," *etc.*, (2 Thess. 3:3), "For he is faithful that has promised," (Heb. 10:23). Memorable is that saying of David—"For you have magnified thy word above all thy name," (Psa. 138:2), which words are to be understood as Ainsworth explains them, *Thy word of promise in Christ, and Thy faithfulness in performing of it, does more exalt Thy name than anything by which Thou art made known.* Oh, then, let all the saints of God, who are heirs of the promises, meditate frequently on the preciousness, freeness, firmness, unchangeableness, and immutability of them.

V. You must meditate on the fullness and richness of the promises are the saints' magazine and spiritual treasure; they are called the "unsearchable riches of Christ," (Eph. 3:6-7). It is one of the greatest titles belonging to a saint to be styled "an heir of the promises," (Heb. 8:17). That man that has a right to all the promises in the Bible is the richest man in the world; for God is his, (and he that has Him that has all things, has all things); Christ is his, (and Christ is all in all); the Spirit is his, (and he who has the Spirit has all good things, as appears by comparing Matt, 7:11 with Luke 11:13). In the first it is said, "How much more shall your Father in heaven give good things," *etc.*; in the second, "How much more shall your heavenly Father give the Holy Spirit," *etc.* Grace and glory, and all outward good things, are His. It is said of the great Duke of Guise, that though he was poor as to his present possessions, yet he was the richest man in France in bills, bonds, and obligations, because he had engaged all the noblemen in France to himself, by preferring of them. A true and real Christian is the richest man in the world in promises and obligations, for he has the great God engaged by promise to be his God, and the God of his. As Charles the First commanded his herald, in a challenge to Francis the First, king of France, to proclaim him with all his titles, styling him Emperor of Germany, King of Castile, Arragon, Naples, Sicily, *etc.* But, Francis commanded his herald to call him so often King of France as the other had titles by all his country; implying that France alone was more worth than all his countries. So when a wicked man brags of his lordships and great possessions, when he boasts of his thousands a year, a child of God may say, God is mine, God is mine, *etc.*; I am richer than all the wicked men in the world.

VI. You must meditate on the latitude and extension or the promises. The promises are the saints' *catholicon* and *panacea.* There is no condition a promises, child of God can be in, but he may find, not only a promise, but a suitable and seasonable promise to comfort him in it And herein especially consists the spiritual excellency and heavenly wisdom of a Christian, not only to study the promises in general, but to labor to find out; and having found out, to meditate on such kind of promises which are most suitable and most seasonable to the condition he is in. As, for example—

If you are poor in estate, meditate on Psa. 34:10; Matt. 6:33; Heb. 13:5.

If barren, and without children, meditate on Isa. 56:5.

If persecuted for Christ's sake, meditate on Matt 5:10; 1 Pet. 4:12-14; Psa. 94:12.

If sick, and under tormenting pains, meditate on Psa. 1.15; Isa. 63:9; Rom. 8:28.

If reproached, slandered, and falsely accused, meditate on Matt 10:25; Matt, 5:11, 12; Luke 6:22, 23.

If Satan tempts you, and you are not able to resist him, meditate on Rom. 19:20; 1 Cor. 10:13; Gen. 3:15; 1 John 3:8.

If your corruptions are too strong for you, meditate on Rom. 6:14; Mic. 7:16.

If God hides His face from you and you sit in darkness, and see no light, meditate on Isa. 1:10, 54:7-8.

If ready to faint in waiting on God, and in expecting the fulfilling of His promises, meditate on Isa. 30:18, 63:3, 40:28-30; Mal. 3:1.

If ready to die, and full of fears and doubts, meditate on 1 Cor. 15:55-57; Hos. 13:14; Rev. 14:13; 1 Cor. 3:22-23, 2 Cor. 5:1, 8.

VII. You must meditate on the variety of the promises, and their difference and distinction one from the other. The promises are like to the stars in the firmament.

1. For their multitude, they are very many. The Scripture is bespangled with promises, as the heavens are with stars. It were happy if the saints would prove spiritual astronomers, and make it their work to study the nature of these stars.

2. For their beauty, excellency, and influence. Every star is beautiful in its kind, and very useful and advantageous; so are the promises. And as the stars are most comfortable in the darkness of the night, so are the promises in the night of trouble and adversity.

3. And especially for their distinction and difference. For as one star differs from another in glory, "There is one glory of, the sun, another of the moon, another of the stars," (1 Cor. 15:41); so do the promises differ exceedingly one from the other in beauty and

excellency. Some are temporal, some spiritual, some of things that are eternal; some are conditional, some absolute; some are promises to those that have grace, some are promises of grace; some are general, others particular; some are original, fundamental, and fountain promises, (as the promise of Jesus Christ, of God being our God, and of the Holy Ghost); others are derivative, and depending promises, (as the promises of all outward comforts here, and of eternal life hereafter). Now it is our duty to take notice of every ray of gold, to meditate on all the promises, both spiritual, temporal, and eternal, both conditional and absolute; both of grace, and to grace, both general and particular; but especially of the original and fundamental promises, the fountain-promises, from whence all others, as so many streams and rivulets, are deduced and derived.

VIII. You must meditate on the usefulness and profitableness of the promises. I have already showed you, that they are the conduits of grace and comfort, that they have a soul-sanctifying and a soul-comforting power. Give me leave to add, that the promises are—

1. The breathings of divine love and affection.
2. The life and soul of faith.
3. The anchor of hope.
4. The wings of prayer.
5. The foundation of industry.
6. The rays and beams of the Sun of Righteousness; and on all these accounts are very useful and advantageous.

1. They are the breathings of divine love and affection. It is an argument of God's wonderful love to His children, that He is pleased to enter into a promise and covenant to be their God, and to give them Christ, and in Christ all blessings here and hereafter. We read,

(Gen. 17:2-3), when God told Abraham that He would make a covenant with him, "he fell on his face as astonished" at so great a mercy, and as thankfully acknowledging the goodness of God towards him. The like we read of David. When God, by Nathan, made a promise to him, he goes into God's house, and prays, "Who am I, O Lord, and what is my house, that the Lord my God should do this?" *etc.* (2 Sam. 7:11, 18-19). The promises are the cabinets of the tender bowels of God; they contain the dear and tender love of God towards His elect children; God, by promising, makes Himself a debtor to them. Now that God, who is bound to none, (no, not to the angels of heaven), should enter into bonds, and bind Himself to give grace and glory to His elect children, this is love above expression! And there is nothing moved God to do this, but, as I have said, His free grace and mercy. For though God be now bound, out of justice and faithfulness, to fulfill His promises, yet nothing moved Him to make these promises but His love and mercy, as David says of what God had promised to him, (2 Sam. 7: 21), "According to thine own heart, and according to thy word, not for any thing in me, for what am I, O Lord," *etc.* So, you see how the promises are the breathings of divine love and affection, and on this account are they very useful and profitable. For love is love's loadstone; therefore the apostle says in 1 John 4:19, "We love him, because he loved us first." The sense of God's love to us will kindle a love in us to God. Even as the beams of the sun reflecting on a wall heats those that walk by the wall, so the beams of God's love shining into our souls warms our hearts with the love of God. "The love of God constrains us," as says Paul, (2 Cor. 5:14). There is a compulsive and constraining power in love. What did not Jacob do for the love of Rachel? How was Mephibosheth affected with the love of David? (2 Sam. 19:8). It is our duty to love those that hate us; but not to love those that love us, is more than heathenish and brutish.

2. They are the life and soul of faith. Faith without a promise to act on is as a body without a soul, as a dead flower which has no beauty or sweetness in it; but faith grounded on the promises will enable a Christian to advance in all manner of holiness. What made Abraham forsake his country and his father's house, and go he knew not whither? Nothing moved him to this, but because God had promised to make him a great nation, and he believed it.

Of all graces, none so casual of holiness as the grace of faith. It is a world overcoming, heart-purifying, life-sanctifying, wonder-working grace; and therefore the promises must needs be very useful, because they are the life and soul of faith.

3. They are the anchor of hope. Hope is called an anchor of the soul (Heb. 6:9), both sure anchor steadfast; but the promises are the anchor of hope. All hope of heaven, which is not founded on a promise, is presumption, and not hope. Presumption is when a man hopes to go to heaven on no ground, or on an insufficient ground. But true hope is a hope grounded on a Scripture promise.

And hope bottomed on divine promises will mightily avail to purity and holiness. Abraham, Isaac, and Jacob lived as pilgrims and strangers on earth, because they looked and hoped for a city which has foundations, whose builder and maker is God, (Heb. 11:9, 10). The Old Testament saints would not accept deliverance on sinful terms, because they hoped for a better resurrection. The Papists and Arminians are much mistaken in teaching that the assurance of salvation is an enemy to godliness. The Scripture says quite the contrary. "He that has this hope, purifies himself, even as he is pure," (1 John 3:3). The true hope of heaven will make us live heavenly.

4. They are the wings of prayer; prayer is a divine cordial to convey grace from heaven into our souls; it is a key to unlock the bowels of mercy which are in God. The best way to obtain holiness is on our knees, the best posture to fight against the devil is on our knees: and therefore prayer is not put as a part of our spiritual armor, but added as that which must be an ingredient in every part, and which will make every part effectual.

But now the promises are the wings of prayer. Prayer without a promise is as a bird without wings: and therefore we read both of Jacob and Jehoshaphat, how they urged God in their prayer with His promises (2 Chron. 20:8-9). And certainly the prayers of the saints, winged with divine promises, will quickly fly up to heaven, and draw down grace and comfort into their souls. And on this account it is that the promises are so useful to a Christian, because they are so helpful in prayer. When we pray we must urge God with His promises, and say, *Lord, have You not said, You will circumcise our hearts to love Thee, You will subdue our sins, You will give the Spirit to those that ask it? Lord, You are faithful, fulfill these Your own promises:* and we must remember this great truth, that the promises God makes to us, to mortify our sins for us, are greater helps against sin than our promises to God to mortify sin. Many men in the day of their distress vow and promise to leave sin and fight against it in the strength of these promises, and instead of conquering sin, are conquered by sin. But if we fight against sin in the strength of Christ and of His promises; if we urge God in prayer with His own word, we shall at last get victory over it, for He has said that "sin shall not have dominion over us," (Rom. 6:14).

5. They are the foundation of industry. The promises do not make men lazy and idle, as some

scandalously say, but they are the ground of all true labor and industry; therefore the. apostle persuades us from the consideration of the promises, to the study of soul-purification, to have our conversation without covetousness (1 Cor. 7:1; Heb. 13:1; 1 Cor. 12:13-14; 2 Cor. 6:17-18); to flee from idolatry, and to separate ourselves from sinful communion. Divine promises are great encouragements to spiritual diligence.

Objection. Though conditional promises be the foundation of industry (because we cannot have the thing promised unless we perform the conditions), yet absolute promises, say some, are foundations of laziness, and therefore, they affirm, there are no absolute promises in Scripture.

Answer. Absolute promises are made foundations of industry in Scripture, as well as conditional. The apostle exhorts us to work out our salvation with fear and trembling, because it is God who works in us both to will and to do of His own good pleasure (Phil. 2:12-13). And the reason is, because God performs nothing which He promises, though never so absolutely, but in the diligent and conscientious use of the means on our part, God promises (Ezek. 36:26) to give us a new heart and a new spirit, *etc.*; but then He adds, (verse 37), "I will yet for this be inquired of by the house of Israel."

6. They are rays and beams, as one says, of Christ the Sun of Righteous, in whom they are founded and established. As all the lines in a circumference, though never so distant, carry a man to one and the same center, so all the promises carry us to Christ the center. For the promises are not made for anything in us, nor have they any stability from us; but they are made in and for Christ to us, to Christ in our behalf, and to us, so far as we are members of Christ. Now, Jesus Christ is the ground of all soul-purification, soul-consolation, and soul-

salvation; and therefore I may safely conclude, that the promises are most singularly useful and advantageous; and that it is the duty of all those that desire to live holily and comfortably, to consider and ponder the profitableness and benefits of the promises.

IX. And lastly, you must meditate of on the great necessity that lies on all men to get a *Scripture interest* in the promises. This I add to awaken Christians to attend diligently to the discourse about the promises, and to show them the necessity of minding and of studying them. For he that has no right to them is in a faithless, hopeless, comfortless, desperate, and damnable condition. All the happiness of a Christian, both here and hereafter, consists especially in his right and title to the promises. The, Scripture tells, us, in express words, that he that is a stranger from the promise is without Christ, without God, without hope (Eph. 2:20). Sad is the condition of that man who has no interest in God nor in Christ, and who is without hope. And such is the condition of him who is a stranger to the promises; for all hope of heaven, which is not bottomed on a promise, is presumption and soul-delusion. All comfort and joy which is not grounded on a promise is soul-cozenage, and all faith not anchored on a promise is nothing else but flattery and soul-mockery. Consider this, you that are full of joy and comfort, and, as you say, rely on Christ for salvation. Tell me, what promise have you to build this faith, this hope, this comfort on? For there are thousands that flatter themselves into hell by a false hope of heaven; thousands, which promise to themselves to go to heaven, but have no promise for it from God. Such were the five foolish virgins, such was the church of Laodicea, such were they mentioned in Matt. 7:24, Hos. 8:2-3, Micah 3:10-11. Remember this, and let it be daily in your thoughts—You that have not true right to the promises, your faith is faction, your hope is presumption, and your joy is delusion. To be a stranger from the promise, is to be without God, without Christ, and without hope. So much for the second particular, *viz.*,—meditate on the promises.

SERMON 5

Psa. 119:92, "Unless thy law had been my delights, I should then have perished in mine affliction."

Now I come to the third and last particular. He that would make the promises as spiritual bladders to keep him from drowning in the deep waters of affliction, must not only make a catalogue of them, and meditate on them, but he must make application of them to his own soul, as belonging to him in particular; he must, as it is said of the godly patriarchs, (Heb. 11:13), be persuaded of them, and embrace them; he must hug and kiss them as his rich portion and glorious inheritance. And this is the chief of all: for no man can receive any comfort from a promise, who is not able to make out his interest in that promise. As the life of a the application of it to ourselves; so the life of a promise is in the appropriation of it What am I the better, says Origen, that Christ took on Him the flesh of a virgin, if He took not my flesh? What was the great prince the better for the miraculous plenty in Samaria, when the prophet told him that he should see it with his eyes, but not eat of it? As the man, who, when he was ready to be drowned, saw a rainbow, (which was a sign that the world should never be again drowned), said, *What am I the better for the rainbow if I perish?*, so may I say, *What is a man the better for the rich mine of treasure contained in the promises, if he has no share in it?*

There are three sorts of professors of religion:—

1. Some lay claim to the promises when they have no right to them; such are your presumptuous sinners who take it for granted that the promises belong to them, who presume themselves into hell by a false hope in the promises; who make a featherbed of the promises, on which they sleep securely in sin. As Thrasilaus, a mad

Athenian, laid claim to every ship that came to Athens, though he had right to none; so a presumptuous sinner lays a claim to every promise, though he has right ta none; he enlarges them beyond their bounds, and makes the conditional promises to be absolute; and such as belong only to those that are in Christ, to belong to him, though he is not in Christ: he sucks the poison of sin and security out of the sweet flowers of the promises.

2. Some have an interest in the promises, and know their interest; these live in heaven while they are on earth; these rejoice in tribulation, and are more than conquerors over the greatest afflictions; these are secure from perishing in the day of distress. That man who, taking the Bible into his hand, can say on right grounds, *All the promises in this book are my portion, and I have a right and title to them*, this man is happy above expression.

3. Some have an interest in the promises, but do not know their interest, and therefore dare not, in the hour of trouble, apply them for their support and consolation. Such are your broken-hearted, wounded, distressed, and deserted Christians: such can receive no comfort from the promises in the day of affliction. When they begin to apply them for their support, the devil suggests to them, and their own doubting hearts tell them, that they misapply them, and that they belong not to them. When a godly minister, whose office is to speak a word in season to those that are weary, (Isa. 1:4), endeavors by the application of the promises to comfort them, their souls refuse to be comforted, they exclude themselves from having a right to Christ and His promises, though Christ would not have them excluded.

They groundlessly fear that their names are written in the black book of reprobation, and that all the curses of the law are their portion; hence it is that they live so uncomfortably and disconsolately in the time of affliction. Now then for the help of such persons, who have a true title to the promises, but know it not, who walk in darkness, and see no light, who believe they are hypocrites, when they are not, and that they are not in Christ, when they are; that I may be God's instrument to enable such to make application of the precious promises to their own souls in particular, in the hour of trouble, for their everlasting support and consolation, I shall lay down these ensuing rules and directions:—

Rule 1. Whosoever in a gospel sense obeys the commanding word of God, has a real interest in the promising word of God. Though you cannot perfectly obey the will of God, yet if you do truly desire and industriously endeavor to obey it in all things; if God has written His law in your heart, and given you a gospel frame, inclining you to the obedience of all His commandments sincerely, though not perfectly, this is an infallible evidence that you have a right and portion in all the promises. This is that which God says, "If ye will obey my voice indeed, then ye shall be a peculiar treasure," *etc.* (Exod. 19:5);—if ye will obey my voice indeed, not only in word and in show, but in deed and in truth. So Jer. 7:5, 7, "If ye thoroughly amend your ways, if ye thoroughly execute judgment, *etc.*, then will I cause you to dwell in this place," *etc.*;—"if ye thoroughly amend," *etc.*, not only in *some* things, but in *all* things; not only *outwardly*, but *inwardly* also. This rule is expressly delivered by the apostle, (1 Tim. 4:8), "Godliness has the promise of the life that now is, and that is to come." If you are a godly man in a gospel sense, that is, one who truly and sincerely endeavors to be godly; if you make God's will your rule to live by, and not your own, God's glory your end, and not your own carnal interest, God's love your principle; if your rules, aims, and principles are godly, all the promises of this life, and of the life to come, belong to thee. It is worth the observing, that all the promises of life and salvation are conditional: happiness is entailed on holiness, glory on grace. You shall read in Ezek. 20:37 of the blessings of the covenant, and of the bond of the covenant; of the blessings of the promise, and of the condition of the promises. If ever you would assure yourselves of your interest in the blessings of the covenant, you must try yourselves by your sincere performance of the condition. So Christ is promised to none but such as believe; pardon of sin to none but such as repent; and heaven to none but such as persevere in well doing. Tell me, then, can you say, as in God's presence, that you have respect to all God's commandments; though you fail in all, yet you have a respect to all; that you obey God in deed and in truth, and that you sincerely labor to be godly? This is a certain sign that all the promises are your portion; but you that are ungodly, and do not thoroughly amend your ways, you that slight, undervalue, and despise the commanding word, you have no part, no portion in the promising word.

But it may be a distressed Christian, though without just cause, will say that he is afraid that he does not sincerely obey the commanding word, and therefore dares not apply to himself the promising word; wherefore I add—

Rule 2. The more you are afraid though you should have no right to the promises, the more right you have, in all probability, to them. This I speak only to the distressed Christian, not that I commend his fear. But this I say, this fear which you are possessed with, is a probable sign that you have an interest in the promises. For a presumptuous sinner never doubts of his right to them, but takes it as a maxim not to be denied that they belong to him. It is a comfortable saying of Mr. Greenham's, when you hear the promises, and are in a cold sweat, and have a fear and a trembling seizing on you lest they should not belong to you, doubt not but that they do belong to thee; for Christ has said in Matthew 11:28, "Come to me, all ye that are weary and heavy laden, and I will give you rest." And the prophet Isaiah in 35:4, calls on those who are of a fearful heart to be strong, and fear not; and tells us, for our comfort, that God will look with an eye of favor on him that is poor, and of a contrite spirit, and trembles at his word (Isa. 66:2).

Rule 3. The more sensible you are of your own unworthiness to lay hold on them. For the promises are, as I have showed, the fruit of free grace. Nothing moved God to enter into covenant with His people, and thereby to become their debtor, but His free love. Free grace brought Christ down from heaven, and it is free grace must carry us up to heaven. Christ Himself is called the gift of God in John 4:10. Moses tells the Israelites, (Deut. 7:7-8), "The Lord did not set his love on you, nor choose you, because you were more in number than any people," *etc.* "But because the Lord loved you, and because he would keep the oath which he had sworn to your fathers, has the Lord brought you out with a mighty hand, and redeemed you," *etc.* God does not love us because we are worthy of His love; but because He loves us, therefore He makes us worthy. We must not bring worthiness to Christ, but fetch worthiness from Christ. And therefore if you are sensible of your own nothingness, emptiness, and unworthiness, lay hold on that excellent promise, "Blessed are the poor in spirit: for theirs is the kingdom of heaven," (Matt. 5:3). Blessed are those who are sensible of their spiritual want, for to them belongs the kingdom of heaven, as certainly as if they were already in it.

Rule 4. Study your interest in the main and fundamental promise, and that will help you to make out your interest in all the others. The main and fundamental promise is the promise of Christ; for all promises, whether spiritual or temporal, are made to us in and through Him. God has promised never to leave us nor forsake us, and that all things shall work together for our good; that is, if we are in Christ. God has said, "All things are ours, whether Paul, or Apollos, whether life or death, whether things present, or things to come," (1 Cor. 3:21-22), but it is with this *proviso*, if we are Christ's. Whosoever takes any comfort from any temporal promise, and is not in Christ, deludes and cheats himself. This then is your work, O Christian: study your interest in Christ, make out that, and make out all. If no interest in Christ, no interest in the promises; if an interest in Christ, an interest in the promises. Let this then be your daily business to make it out to your soul, that Christ is yours.

Question. How shall I be able to do this?

Answer. For this purpose you must diligently study three things—

1. The universality of the promise of Christ
2. The freeness of it.
3. The condition on which He is tendered.

1. The universality of the promise of Christ. Christ Jesus, with all His benefits promised to everyone who is willing to lay hold on Him, as He is tendered in the gospel. The apostles are commanded to go into all the world, and to preach the gospel to every creature, "He that believeth and is baptized, shall be saved," *etc.*, If you have a heart to believe, though your sins are so great, it is for the honor of Jesus Christ to pardon them. As the sea covers great rocks as well as small, so the mercy of God in Christ will pardon great sins, as well as little. It will cost Christ as little to wash away the guilt of great sins as of small. Christ is a great physician. And David prays, "Pardon my iniquity, for it is great," (Psa. 25:11). Though your sins be never so bloodily

circumstantiated, though never so often reiterated, though you are never so loathsome, yet if you cannot believe, there is a fountain opened to the house of David, and to the inhabitants of Jerusalem, for sin and for uncleanness; and therefore let no man exclude himself from a right to Christ, who is willing to take Christ on Christ's terms. He that excludes himself, offers the greatest injury imaginable.

First, to Jesus Christ, for he makes Him a liar. Christ has said in John 6:37, "If any man come to me, I will in no wise cast him out;" and he says, Christ will cast me out, although I do come to Him.

Secondly, to his own soul, for he necessitates himself to damnation; for Christ has said expressly, "He that believeth not shall be damned."

Objection. But I am afraid that I am a reprobate, and that God has excluded me from having an interest in Christ. *Answer.* Who told you so? It is one great sign you are not, because the devil would persuade you that you are. But, however, secret things belong to God; but those things which are revealed, to us and our children. God has kept the black book of reprobation secret. He opens the whole book of election to some of His children, but He keeps His black book unrevealed. It is a sin for any man to think himself a reprobate, (unless he can prove that he has sinned the sin against the Holy Ghost), for this thought would hinder him from the use of means for his salvation, and cause him to despair, which is a sin of the first magnitude; and therefore take heed of complimenting yourself into hell by a sinful modesty, in refusing to believe in Christ. Take heed of dallying or delaying in the great work of laying hold on Christ on Christ's terms. Remember God excludes none from Christ, but such as exclude themselves by unbelief. And remember, "Whosoever believeth not the Son, shall not see life, but the wrath of God abideth on him."

2. You must study the freeness of the promise of Christ. God promises Jesus Christ—"Ho everyone that thirsteth, come ye to the waters, and he that has no money; come ye, buy, and eat, yes, come buy wine and milk without money, and without price," *etc.*

Christ is offered in the gospel, without price, without merit, and without any motive inducing on our parts (Rev. 22:17; Isa. 55:1.). Therefore the Holy Ghost says, "Whosoever will, let him take the water of life freely." Do not let your undeservedness hinder you from laying hold on Christ as you portion. Do not say, *I am not worthy that Christ should own me*. Christ will own thee, not because you are worthy, but because He delights in mercy, (Mic. 7:18). Do not say, *I am not humbled enough, and therefore I dare not lay hold on Christ,* for humiliation is not required to make us precious to Christ, but to make Christ precious to us; and if you are so far humbled, as to be willing to take Christ on Christ's terms, you are humbled enough, to divine acceptation, though not to divine satisfaction. Every stung Israelite, who was enabled to look up to the brazen serpent, was healed, though he was not stung to that proportion that another Israelite was.

3. You must study the condition on which Christ is promised. It is certain Christ is not tendered absolutely, without any condition. Christ is not offered to a proud sinner, resolving so to continue, or to a drunkard, resolving to persevere in his drunkenness. Those texts which declare the freeness of the offer of Christ, also mention a condition to be performed by those that will have Him, (Rev. 22:17; Isa. 55:1). In both places the condition of thirsting is expressed: "Let him that is athirst come," "Ho every one that thirsteth…"

Question. Does not the mentioning of a condition take away the freeness of the tender of Christ?

Answer. By no me*Answer.* The reason is, because

this very condition is the free gift of God. The apostle says, (Rom. 4:16), "Therefore it is of faith, that it might be by grace." The condition of faith does not make the offer of Christ not to be of grace: but therefore it is of faith, that it might be of grace; for as Christ, so also faith is the gift of God.

We do not preach conditions to justification in a Popish sense, as if they merited out of congruity the pardon of sin; or in an Arminian sense, as if we could do anything by our free-will, without grace, to dispose ourselves to justification; but in *a Scripture sense* we say, that all those on whom God intends to bestow Christ freely, He freely opens their eyes to see their undone condition out of Christ. He humbles them under the sense of their sad condition, and out of His free mercy enables them by faith to lay hold on Christ, and to receive of Him on His own terms. Faith is not the cause for which, but the cause *without* which, God will not give us Christ.

Question. But what is the condition on which Christ is promised?

Answer. There is, if I may so speak, the condition required to the preparing and disposing us for an interest in Christ, and the condition applying Christ to us, and bringing Him into our possession.

1. The condition required to the disposing, preparing, and fitting us for an interest in Christ. And this is the sight of our sins, the sense of them, and a real willingness to part with them. There is no man qualified, according to the gospel, to rest on Christ for pardon of his sins, who is not really willing to part with them. And no man will be willing to part with his sins, which he naturally loves as himself, unless he see the sinfulness and cursedness of them, and feels in some measure the smart of them. The woman who had the bloody issue never thought of coming to Christ until all her money

was spent in vain among other physician. The prodigal child would never have returned to his father, had he not seen himself utterly undone by wandering from him.

2. The condition applying Christ to us, and bringing Him in to our possession. This is faith, which therefore is the proper condition of the gospel, on which Christ is tendered. Now this faith is not a bare receiving and taking of Christ; for there are many who take Him, and mistake Him. There is no man but is willing when he is dying to take Christ, as the men of the old world were willing to go into the ark when the flood came. But this taking and receiving of Christ, if it be right, has six properties:—

(1.) It is a receiving of Christ with all His legal rights: Christ *and* disgrace *and* reproach *and* poverty, Christ *and* His cross. There are many would be glad of Christ, but they will not take up His cross. They would take Christ down from the cross, as Joseph of Arimathea did, and leave the cross behind them. But he that takes Christ aright will be as willing to wear a crown of thorns for His sake as a crown of gold.

(2.) It is a receiving of Christ in all His offices, as our King, Priest, and Prophet. A true believer is as willing to receive Christ into his soul, as he is that Christ should receive him into heaven; he is as willing to have Christ reign over him, as he is to reign with Christ in heaven. He desires not only to be saved, but to be healed by Christ.

(3.) It is a receiving of Christ into every room of the soul; for Christ will come into every room, or into never a room. A true believer opens every door to Christ; he gives Him the lock and key of the whole man, and desires that He would come and reside in every room.

(4.) It is a receiving of Christ, and Him only. For Christ must rule alone, or not at all. A hypocrite would compound with Christ, and, like the false mother, divide the child; but a true believer says with the prophet, "O Lord our God, other lords besides thee have had dominion over us; but now by thee only will we make mention of thy name," And with the true mother he will give the whole to God.

(5.) It is a receiving of Christ in health as well as in sickness; in prosperity as well as in adversity; in youth as well as in old age; in life as well as in death. Most people make use of Christ, merely as a shelter against a storm, for their own ends, (as the Athenians did of Themistocles), and when the storm is over, forsake Him. Most people fly to Christ in their distress, as Joab did to the horns of the altar; and when they can serve the devil no longer, then they begin to think of serving of God. But a true believer will give his best days to God as well as his worst; he desires not only to die in Christ, but to *live* for Christ; he receives Christ in health, *etc.*

(6.) It is a receiving of Christ, not only for an hour, or a day, or a year, but forever. True faith marries the soul to Christ which is never to part. Once a Christian is a member of Christ, he is forever a member.

Now, there is no child of God, of what size soever, (though he be but as a toe in Christ's body), who cannot truly say that he is willing to receive Jesus Christ with all these properties, to receive all Christ, with all His appurtenances, and to receive Him only, in every room, in health, and forever. And therefore do not let the devil, or your misgiving heart, or your melancholy fancy, keep you off from believing that Christ Jesus is your portion, and that you have an interest in the main and fundamental promise, and by that in all the others. Do to Christ as the Shunammitish woman did to the prophet (2 Kings 4:30), lay fast hold on Him, and suffer not the devil to cause you to let go of your hold. Oh that there might be this day a blessed and happy marriage between Jesus Christ and every distressed Christian.

Objection. But suppose I am willing to take Christ on Christ's terms, can I rest assured that Christ will receive me?

Answer. Yes, doubtless. For He has in John 6:37 said He will, and He is truth itself, and cannot lie. Indeed, a poor wounded sinner will sometimes confess that he is willing with all his heart to receive Christ on His own terms; but he is afraid lest Christ should refuse to receive him.

But this is a needless fear, for Christ will in no wise refuse those that come to Him (John 1:12). To as many as receive Him, to all those He will give power to become the sons of God, even to them that believe on His name (John 5:24). He that believes has everlasting life, and shall never come into condemnation, but is passed from death to life. So much for the fourth rule.

If these rules and directions already named will not enable you to apply the promises, so as to keep you from perishing in the day of distress, let me add—

Rule 5. If you cannot lay hold upon the promises made to those who are in the highest form in Christ's school, lay hold on the promises made to those who are in the lower forms. In Christ's school there are divers sorts of scholars; some are in the high form, some in the middle, some in the lowest; some are babes in Christ's school, some are grown Christians; some are as tall cedars, some are as low shrubs. Now you must know that it is our duty to labor to be of the highest form. He that says he has grace enough, has grace little enough. He that stints himself in his endeavors after grace, never had true grace. We must labor to be perfect as God is perfect. But yet you must also know, that he that is a real scholar in Christ's school is in a happy condition, though he is not the best scholar; and that it is our duty so to eye the eminent graces which are in others as to be thereby incited to a further progress in grace, but not so as to be thereby disheartened and discouraged. There are many distressed Christians like to those who gaze so long on the brightness of the sun, that when they come into their houses they cannot see at all—they pour so much on the transcendent excellences which are in their brethren, that they are stark blind in their own concernments, and cannot see any grace in themselves, and hereon are apt to conclude that they are out of God's favor. But this is a non sequitur. The foot must not say that it is no part of the body, because it is not so eminent a part as the head or heart We must rather say with the martyr, "Blessed be God that I am a member in Christ's body, though but the weakest and lowest." We must not rest satisfied with being low Christians; but yet we must not therefore say, *we are no Christians.* And when we are under great tribulations and temptations, if we cannot apply to ourselves for our comfort those promises which are made to eminent saints of the highest form, let us apply those which are made to true saints, though to such as are the lowest of the lowest form; and hereby we shall, through God's blessing, find our souls marvelously supported and comforted. As, for example, Christ has said, "Blessed are the poor in spirit, for theirs is the kingdom of heaven." And, therefore, though, you are not rich in grace, yet if poor in spirit, you are blessed (Matt. 5:3). Christ says, "Blessed are they that mourn, for they shall be comforted." Though you cannot live without sin, yet if a mourner for your own and other men's sins, you are blessed (Matt. 5:4).

Christ says, "Blessed are they which do hunger and thirst after righteousness." Though you find an exceedingly great want of righteousness in you, yet if you hunger and thirst after it, you are blessed (Matt. 5:6).

Christ says, "Come to me all ye that labor and are heavy laden, and I will give you rest," (Matt. 11:28). This text is an alabaster box full of precious consolation. If you sins are a burden to you, Christ will give you rest; if you carry them about you, not as a golden chain about your neck, but as an iron chain about your feet; if you are heavy laden with them, Christ will take them off your shoulders, and put them on His.

Christ says that He will not break the bruised reed, nor quench the smoking flax, until He sends forth judgment to victory. If you have grace as a smoking flax, Christ will not quench it, but assist it, until it becomes a great flame.

Christ says that the whole have no need of the physician, but they that are sick, and that He came not to call the righteous, but sinners to repentance. If you are a sin-sick sinner, your name is in Christ's commission— He came to save you.

Christ says, "The Son of man is come to save that which was lost." If you apprehend yourself to be in a lost condition, you are among the number of those whom Christ came to save.

The apostle says, "There is no condemnation to those who are in Christ, who walk not after the flesh, but after the Spirit," (Rom. 8:1). Though you have much flesh in you, and are sometimes overtaken with sin, yet if you do not walk after the flesh, as a servant after his master, if you walk after the Spirit, there is no condemnation to you.

The apostle says, "If we confess our sins, God is faithful to forgive us our sins, and to cleanse us from all unrighteousness," (1 John 1:9). If we confess our sins, out of a detestation of sin, with bleeding hearts, and a sincere purpose of forsaking them, God is bound by virtue of His promise to forgive us, else He would be unfaithful.

The apostle says, that "He that has begun a good work in us, will perform it until the day of Jesus Christ,"

(Phil. 1:6). And therefore if you have truth of grace, though but as a grain of mustard-seed, do not doubt but that God, in the diligent use of means, will enable you to persevere.

Rule 6. If you cannot apply to yourself your comfort in affliction the conditional promises, lay hold on the absolute promises. I have formerly told you that there are some promises conditional, others absolute; some to grace, others of grace, some to those that are godly, others to make us godly. God has not only promised to pardon those that repent, but to give repentance; not only to justify those that believe, (Acts 5:21; Phil. 1:29; Deut. 30:6; Jer. 32:40) but to give us to believe; not only to give heaven to those that love Him, but to give us grace to love Him; not only to save those that persevere, but to enable us to persevere; and, therefore, if you cannot lay hold on the promises to those that are godly, apply those which are made to make us godly. If not those which are made to those that repent, believe, and persevere, apply those wherein God promises to give us to repent, believe, and persevere. If not the conditional, lay hold on the absolute.

There are these differences and agreements between conditional and absolute promises—

1. For conditional promises.

(1.) All promises of life and salvation are conditional.

(2.) Conditional promises are the fruit of free grace, as well as absolute. It is free grace which enables us to perform the conditional, and free grace which moved God to promise such great mercies on such conditions.

(3.) They are the fruit of rich grace and rare mercy, as well as absolute promises.

(4.) They are of great use to quicken a lazy Christian, and to encourage him to diligence; for no man can obtain the blessing promised, but he that performs the conditions enjoined.

(5.) They are rare touchstones to try our interest in the promises; for he that neglects to perform the condition cannot challenge an interest in the blessing promised on the performing of it.

2. For absolute promises,

(1.) Though promises to grace be conditional, yet promises of grace are absolute, and are made by God to Christ in the behalf of His elect children, according to that of David, "Ask of me, and I shall give thee the heathen for thine inheritance, and the uttermost parts of the earth for thy possession."

(2.) There are no promises so absolute as to exclude all endeavors on our part. God will do the things promised for us, but by us. We work, but it is God who works all our works in us and for us.

(3.) Absolute promises are foundations of industry, as well as conditional. The truth of this I made out in the former sermon.

(4.) Absolute promises are demonstrative arguments of special election, and of the perseverance of the saints. There are some peculiar ones to whom God has promised, in the use of means, absolutely to write His law in their hearts, to cause them to walk in His ways, to give them infallibly and infrustrably repentance, faith, and perseverance. The promise of the first grace, and of the crowning grace, is absolute. And therefore the doctrine of special election, and of perseverance, must needs be true.

(5.) Absolute promises are mighty helps to wounded consciences, and rare cordials for fainting and despairing Christians. When you are in the dark, and see no light, fly from the conditional promises to the absolute; say, Lord, You have not only promised to give pardon to those who repent, but You have exalted

Christ for to give repentance; You have not only promised *to justify those who believe, but to give grace to believe. Lord fulfill Thine own promise to Thy servant, etc.*

Objection. All my fear is that these absolute promises do not belong to me.

Answer. Take heed of making desperate conclusions against yourself. Say as the King of Nineveh, "Who knoweth but God may turn and have mercy?" Do not exclude yourself. Neither man nor angel can say you are excluded. No man ought to believe himself to be a reprobate (as I have showed); these promises belong to all that can lay hold on them as they are tendered. As the brazen serpent belonged to all those who were able to look on it, so do these promises to all that can by faith look up, that they may be healed. Say as the four lepers in another case, *If I go on in unbelief, I am certainly damned, and therefore I will venture on Christ, I will fly to this ark, and if I perish, I perish believing,* (2 Kings 7).

If these directions will not suffice to comfort you in the day of adversity, let me add—

Rule 7. All promises made in Scripture to the saints in general are applicable to every saint in particular. God promised to Solomon, (1 Kings 8:37, 40), and Jehoshaphat applied this to his own particular condition, (2 Chron. 20:9). God promises to the saints in general that He will give them grace and glory; that He will withhold no good thing from them; that they shall want nothing that is good; and that all outward blessings shall be added to them (Psa. 48:10; 43:10; Matt. 6:33). Now, there is no saint but he may as justly lay hold on those promises as if his name were named in them; and the reason is, because all the promises do meet in Christ, as all lines in a center.

And every saint has all Christ And therefore promises made to those that are in Christ belong to all that are in Christ.

Rule 8. All promises made to particular saints are applicable to all saints in the same condition. God promises by Joshua, that He would never leave him nor forsake him (Joshua 5; Heb. 13:5). This is applied by the apostle for the comfort of every saint. Christ tells Peter, in Luke 22:33, "I have prayed for thee, that thy faith fail not." This is applicable to every saint. Christ prays for you and me, and therefore he adds, "When thou are converted strengthen thy brethren." Therefore the apostle Paul says that God comforted him in his tribulation that he might be able to comfort those who are in trouble by the comfort wherewith he was comforted (2 Cor. 1:4). And the apostle James propounds the example of the prophets in general, and of Job in particular, to persuade to patience in affliction (James 5:10-11). And therefore when you are in any strait, consider what God has promised to others in your condition, and what God has done to them He will do to you, for He is unchangeable. And do not say, if I were a Paul, a Peter, or a Job, God would do to me as He did to them; but I am a poor, weak, unworthy creature, not worthy to be named in the day which these are named. But consider, if you are a member of Christ's body, (though but as the toe), Christ will have a care of thee. If a child of God, (though but weak and sickly), your heavenly Father will provide for you. A father is tender of every child, and a man of every member of his body; so will God be of all those who belong to Him, though but babes in Christ,

Rule 9. The promises of the gospel are all connected. If you have a true right to any one promise to which promises, heaven is annexed, you have a right to all the others. As the commandments of God are chained together, he that breaks one breaks all, and he that sincerely labors to keep one will labor to keep all, according to that rule, *Whatsoever is done for God is done equally.*

And as the graces of God are linked together, (and therefore heaven is sometimes promised to our grace, because he that has one saving grace has all), so also are the promises joined together —he that has a right to one has a right to all. For they are all but one and the same for substance. They are all the fruit of the same free love in God.

They are all the branches of the same covenant of grace, (and therefore if you have a right to the covenant, you have a right to all the promises); they all carry us to Christ and meet in Christ, and are in Him, "Yes," and in Him "Amen." And therefore if you have a right to Christ, you have a right to all.

This is a point of singular comfort in the worst of days and dangers; for sometimes a child of God under great afflictions can lay hold on one promise and not on another, and some can apply those which others cannot, and others those which they cannot. Let all such know for their great comfort, that he that has right to one branch of the covenant has right to all. He that has let fall a chain of gold, consisting of divers links, into the water, if he can catch hold on any one of the links, he will easily get out the whole chain. The promises are like to a golden chain with divers links; lay hold on one aright, and this will assure you of your interest in all the rest.

I have known many, yes, very many, who have died with a great deal of comfort from the application of that one text to their own condition, "We know that we have passed from death to life, because we love the brethren," (John 3:14). When all other evidences failed them, and all other texts of Scripture afforded them no comfort, here they anchored, here they found rest for their souls. They blessed God that they could say, that they loved the brethren, and loved them not for any outward respect, but because of the image of God in them, and they loved them when poor, as well as when rich; and the more they had of God, the more they loved them; and they loved them even when they were reproved by them of their faults. And on this one plank they swam safely and comfortably to the haven of eternal happiness.

Rule 10. If your condition be so sad, your melancholy so excessive, that you cannot lay hold on any promise, yet notwithstanding look towards it; say, as Jonah when he was in the whale's belly, "Then I said I am cast out of thy sight, yet I will look again towards thy holy temple," (Jonah 2:4). The temple was a type of Christ. Though, you cannot apply Christ to your soul for your comfort, yet look towards Him; and if you cannot come to Him, He will come to you: if you cannot apprehend Him, He will apprehend you. As the loadstone will draw the iron, though the iron cannot draw the loadstone (Psa. 3:12); so will Christ (your heavenly loadstone) draw you to the promise, though you cannot draw yourself to it. "No man can come to me," says Christ, "except the Father draw him," (John 6:44); pray therefore with the Church, (Song of Songs 1:4), "Draw me, and we will run after thee."

Rule 11. Pray to God to give you spiritual eyes to behold your interest in the promises. For as it is God who makes them, so it is only He who can irradiate them, and open your eyes to see your right in them. It is with promises, as I have said, as with chapters and sermons; a man may read a chapter, and hear a sermon, and taste no sweetness in them at one time, and at another time taste much sweetness in them, as God is pleased to cooperate with the reading of the one, and hearing of the other.

So it is with the promises, and therefore pray to God to enlighten your eyes, that you do not sleep the sleep of death (Psa. 12:3). Pray to Christ to anoint your eyes with His spiritual eye-salve (Rev. 3:18); and to cause you to hope in His word of promise; according to that excellent prayer of David, "Remember the word to thy servant, on which you have caused me to hope." It is God must cause us to hope and trust in His promises, or else we shall never be able (Psa. 119:49). God has given you eyes to see your misery; oh pray for eyes to see His mercy. The church of Laodicea wanted eyes to see her misery; she was miserable, and naked, and did not know it (Rev. 3:16). You have eyes to see your undone condition out of Christ; pray for eyes to behold the riches of mercy that are in Christ, and His willingness to receive all that come to Him.

Rule 12. Pray to God, not only to give you spiritual eyes, to see your interest in the promises, but a spiritual hand, to enable you to apply them to your own soul in particular. By this spiritual hand, I mean, a Christ-appropriating faith. Justifying faith is, as it were, the hand of the soul, by which we appropriate Christ, and all the promises, as belonging to us in particular. Now faith is the gift of God. Pray for the spirit of faith (Eph. 2:8). And for your encouragement, consider, that the Spirit is called the promise of the Father, and that Holy Spirit of promise (Acts 1:4): And God has promised to give the Spirit to those who ask for it (Eph. 1:13):—"If ye then being evil, know how to give good gifts to your children; how much more shall your heavenly Father give the Holy Spirit to them that ask him?" The office of the Holy Spirit is first to seal grace, and then to seal to grace: first, the Spirit sanctify us; then it witnesses to our spirits that we are sanctified. Pray therefore to God (Eph. 1:14) that He would not only work grace in you, but witness to the grace which He has wrought.

Pray for the sanctifying and sealing work of the Spirit, that He would not only fit you to have an interest in the promises, but assure you of your interest in them.

Rule 13. Study your interest in the promises in the time or health and outward prosperity, for I find by experience that a child of God, under outward affliction, or divine desertion, or extreme melancholy, is many times like a man in the dark. A man in the dark cannot, though never so learned, read in a book of the clearest print or fairest characters; he cannot, though never so active, undertake anything of weight.

No more can a child of God in the hour of distress read his evidences for heaven, much less study to find out evidences; he looks on all the promises with a black pair of spectacles, and wants light to see his interest in them. When Zion was in distress she said, "God had forsaken her, and her Lord had forgotten her," (Isa. 59:1). When David was persecuted by Saul, he said in his haste, "All men were liars," (Psa. 116:1) even Samuel himself, who had told him that God would bestow the kingdom on him. He said in his haste he was cut off from before God's eyes (Psa. 31:22; 88:13-18). So did Haman. Christ himself when He was on the cross, with a loud voice said, "My God, my God, why hast thou forsaken me?" As men in shivering fits and fevers are not fit judges of meats and drinks, whether they be good or bad, because their palates are out of taste; so a distressed Christian, when under extreme melancholy, divine desertion, or some great affliction, is no fit judge at such a time of his interest in the promises. And therefore my advice is, make out your interest in time of prosperity, and lean on it in time of adversity. Make and read over your evidences for heaven in time of health, and learn them by heart, that when you come into a dark condition, you may neither have them to make or to read. Do as Tamar did, (Gen. 38:18-25). When Judah, her father-in-law, lay with her, she took as a pledge his signet, bracelets, and staff; and afterwards, when she was in great distress, and ready to be burnt as a harlot, she then brought her staff, and signet, and bracelets, and said, "By the man whose these are am I with child and thereby she saved her life. So must you do in time of health, study your interest in the promises, and in time of sickness live on what you have studied, then bring forth your staff and bracelets, *etc.* Then produce your evidences, and make use of them, as spiritual buttresses to keep you from falling into despair.

I knew a very godly woman, not unknown to many here, who in her lifetime had taken a great deal of pains to compose and write down her evidences for heaven, and who also kept a diary of her life, and wrote down how she spent every day. When she lay on her deathbed, it pleased God to withdraw Himself from her for a while, and to let the devil loose, who tempted her to despair, told her she was a hypocrite, a formalist, and that she had no true grace in her. She sent for me, made her bitter complaint to me, and sadly bewailed her condition. Then she told me, which before I did not know, how she had spent her life, how careful she had been in searching her ways, in observing how she spent every day, and how exact in collecting evidences for heaven. The book was sent for, I read a great part of it to her, and took much delight and content in what I read. And it pleased God to come to her with comfort in the reading of it. She showed her staff and her bracelets, and thereby quenched the fiery darts of the devil.

So, I have in three sermons taught you how to make use of Scripture promises, as conduits of soul-support and soul-consolation in the day of distress. When you hereafter read the Bible, remember the promising word, as well as the commanding and threatening word; make a catalogue of the promises, meditate on the preciousness, freeness, usefulness, latitude, richness, and immutability of them. They are as certain as God himself; they have the strength of God, the comforts of God, and assistance of God in them; above all, labor to make application of them to your own soul. For this purpose, study these thirteen rules and directions. Pray to God to give you spiritual eyes to see your interest in them, and spiritual hands to reach out after them. Pray to God to give you spiritual ability, to act faith on the promises, to draw virtue from them, as the woman who had the bloody issue did from Christ; to suck out all the sweetness that is in them, to hang on them, as the woman did on the prophet, and as the bee does on a flower; and by application of them to your soul to live in God and on God here, until you come to enjoy the blessings promised with God forever in heaven.

There is one objection behind, which, when I have answered, I have done. For a distressed Christian will object, and say—

Objection. Though the promises are rare cordials, and shall all of them be certainly fulfilled, yet God is oftentimes long before He fulfills them; and while God is fulfilling of His promises, I may in the meantime perish in my afflictions.

Answer. It cannot be denied but that God is oftentimes very long in fulfilling His promises (Gen. 3:15; Luke 18:7-8). He promised that the seed of the woman should bruise the serpent's head, but it was four thousand years before that promise was actually accomplished. He promises to avenge His elect of all their enemies; to do it speedily; and the souls under the altar cry, "How long, O Lord, holy and true, dost thou not judge and avenge our blood on them that dwell on the earth?" (Rev. 6:10). But this is not yet fulfilled.

No, I must add, that God is not only a long time performing His promises, but sometimes, instead of performing them, He seems to the eye of flesh and blood to walk contrary to them. Sometimes the providences of

God run cross to His promises. God promised to make David king: instead of this, he is persecuted by Saul as a partridge on the mountains; he is driven to that extremity, that he begins to doubt of God's promise, and to say that one day he should die by the hand of Saul. God promised to Joseph that the sun, moon, and stars should worship him, and that his sheaf should be lifted up above the sheaves of his brethren (Gen. 37:9). But he finds the quite contrary: his brethren seek to slay him, sell him into Egypt, and there he is put in prison as one quite forsaken of God. But yet notwithstanding all this, you must know that though the way of God in performing His promises be very mysterious and secret, yet He will at last perform every iota and tittle of them. So David was at last made king of Israel, and Joseph lord of Egypt, and his brethren came all to worship him.

Question. How must we carry and behave ourselves at such times, when providences seem to run cross to God's promises?

Answer. At such times there are three things required of us:—

1. It is our duty to wait patiently and believingly until providences and promises meet together. He that believes, does not make haste. The prophet there speaks of a glorious promise, and adds, that a true saint will wait God's time, which is the most fit and best time; he will patiently expect until God fulfills His promise; he will do as the martyr did, who might have escaped privately out of prison, and was tempted to it by his friends, but answered, he would not go out of prison when his enemies would have him, for they would make him tarry longer than he should, nor yet when his friends would have him, for they would make him tarry a lesser time then he should; but he would come out when God would have him. God's time is the best, and they are soon enough delivered, who are delivered in God's way,

and at God's time. This then is your great duty, O Christian,—to wait patiently, and believingly, and not to seek by unlawful ways to be rid of your miseries, as David did by going to the Philistines; and as many in Queen Mary's days did, by yielding to the Popish superstitions. To help you to wait God's leisure, holding faith and a good conscience, you have—

(1.) Many rare and precious promises made to those that wait on Him; which I have formerly named.

(a.) You have four attributes in God to support you—His faithfulness, almightiness, infinite goodness, and wisdom. He is faithful, and not one tittle of His Word shall fall to the ground: He is almighty, and able to do whatsoever he has promised; He is infinitely wise, to know the best time and season, and infinitely good and loving to His children, and does not willingly afflict them, but will make haste to help them (Lam. 3:35).

2. It is our duty to live on promises, while providences seem to run cross to promises. This is the meaning of Hab. 2:4, "The just shall live by faith." They shall live by faith; when they have nothing else to live on, when sense and reason tell them they are undone, then shall they live by faith in the promises, and not only live patiently, but comfortably, and joyfully as the same prophet says, (Hab. 3:17-19), "Although the fig-tree shall not blossom, neither shall fruit be in the vine, and the field shall yield no meat," *etc.* "Yet I will rejoice in the Lord! I will joy in the God of my salvation." This life Paul lived, when the ship in which he was, was ready to be drowned, when there was neither sunlight, nor starlight, yet he was exceedingly cheerful, because God had promised to preserve him, and those with him, By living this life, God is much honored, and our souls much quieted and refreshed (see Acts 17:20, 23-24).

3. It is our duty to continue praying until providences and promises meet together. For it is prayer,

and prayer only, which will at last reconcile God's promises, and God's dispensations, and cause them to meet and to kiss one another; for as the promises are the ground and rule of our prayers, so our prayers are the divine ways and means for the obtaining of the promises. I say as the promises are—

(1.) The ground of our prayers. For we cannot pray in faith, unless we have some promise to bottom our prayers on; therefore David often charges God in his prayers with His promise. He harps eight times on the same string in one psalm, to teach us, that the greatest rhetoric and oratory we can use in our prayers, is to urge God with His promise (Psa. 119:28, 38, 41, 65, 76, 107, 142, 149).

(2.) They are not only the ground, but the *rule* of our prayers. As we must pray for nothing but what God has promised, so we must regulate our prayers according to God's promises. Those things which He has absolutely promised, we must pray for absolutely; and where God has put conditions and exceptions, there our prayers must be conditional.

Now as the promises are the ground and rule of our prayers, so our prayers are divine means and helps for the obtaining of the promises. Though God has made many glorious and precious promises to His children, yet He will perform none of them, but to those who by prayer seek them at His hands. When Nathan told David what great things God had promised to him, he went into God's house to pray for them, (2 Sam. 7). The prophet Isaiah mentions a glorious promise, (Isa. 53:25); but he adds, "Put me in remembrance," (verse 20). So, (Ezek. 36:37), "I will yet for this be inquired of by the house of Israel;" and therefore when you read the promises of the Bible, remember whatsoever God makes a promise, you must make a prayer, and that prayer will quicken the fulfilling of the promises. You must continue to pray, and not faint: for the vision is but for an appointed time; though it tarry, wait for it, because it will surely come, it will not tarry. This Daniel did, when he understood the time approached, *etc.* He prayed, (Dan. 9:2, 3). As did David, (Psa. 56:9-10; 57:1-2). So you must do as well. These are the three great duties which the Lord requires of us at all times, but more especially in these our days, wherein the providences of God seem to run quite cross to His promises. The Lord give us grace to practice them. So much for this text.

FINIS

TREMBLING FOR THE ARK OF GOD

1 Samuel 4:13, "And when he came, lo, Eli sat upon a seat by the wayside, watching; for his heart trembled for the ark of God."

This sermon was preached December 28, 1662.

That you may better understand these words, you must know that whatsoever God threatened against old Eli, in the second and third chapters, because he did not restrain his wicked sons from their lewd courses, is here executed in this chapter. Therefore we read there were four thousand Israelites slain by the Philistines. The elders of Israel met together to consult how to repair this great loss; they confess it was the Lord that had smitten them. For they say, "Wherefore hath the Lord smitten us today before the Philistines?" And they conclude, the way to repair this their loss was to fetch the ark of the covenant of the Lord from Shiloh, and carry it into the battle. Whereupon they appointed Hophni and Phinehas to fetch it, for they imagined that the presence of the ark would save them from ruin.

But here, they were miserably mistaken. For this judgment came, not because the ark was not in the camp, but because their sin *was in the camp*. The ark of the covenant would not preserve those that had broken covenant with God. And therefore there was a great slaughter of the Israelites; thirty thousand men were slain, Hophni and Phinehas were also slain, and the ark itself was taken prisoner. But what was old Eli doing? He was ninety-eight years old, and was not able to go to the battle, but sits on a seat by the wayside near the battle; and there he sits, thinking what shall become of the ark. "And lo, Eli sat upon a seat by the wayside, watching; for his heart trembled for the ark of God," for fear lest the ark should be taken. He was not troubled what should become of his two sons, or what should become of the people of Israel, but what should become of the *ark of God.*

In the words of the text are three parts:

1. Old Eli's concern for the ark,
2. Old Eli's trembling for fear of the ark,
3. Old Eli's preferring the safety of the ark before the safety of his two sons, wife and children.

"He sat upon a seat by the wayside watching; for his heart trembled for the ark of God." But what was the ark of God? Why should old Eli's heart tremble for fear of the ark?

I answer, this ark was the holiest of all the things of God; it was so holy that it made every place holy where it came. "And Solomon brought up the daughter of Pharaoh, out of the city of David, into the house that he had built for her, for he said, My wife shall not dwell in the house of David king of Israel, because the places are holy whereunto the ark of the Lord hath come," (2 Chronicles 8:11). This ark was the dwelling-place of God, it was the habitation of God. "The Lord reigneth...He sitteth between the cherubims," (Psalm 99:1). Now these cherubims were placed over the ark; it was the speaking place of God, He met his people there, and there He gave and answer to them. "And thou shalt put the mercy-seat above upon the ark; and in the ark thou shalt put the testimony that I shall give thee: and there I will meet with thee, and I will commune with thee from above the mercy-seat, from between the two cherubims which are upon the ark of the testimony, of all things which I will give thee in commandment unto the children of Israel," (Exodus 25:21-22). This ark was God's foot-stool, and all the people of God worship Him before the foot-stool of God. "Exalt ye the Lord our God, and worship at His foot-stool, for He is holy," (Psalm 99:5). The ark was also the glory and the strength of Israel. "And he delivered his strength into captivity, and his glory into the enemy's hand," (Psalm 78:61). It was the terror of the enemies of God, and therefore when the ark came into the battle, the Philistines were afraid, and said "Woe unto us, for God is come into the camp." And indeed this ark was called Jehovah. "And it came to pass, when the ark set forward, that Moses said, "Rise up, Lord, and let thine enemies be scattered:" and when it rested, he said, "Return, O Lord, unto the many thousands of Israel," (Numbers 10:35). In a word, *the ark was a pledge and visible sign of God's gracious presence with his people.* As long as the ark was safe, they were safe; and when the ark was with them, then God's presence was with them. But when the ark was gone, God was gone—His comforting presence, His protecting presence, and His preserving presence.

It is therefore no wonder that this good old man sat watching here for fear of the ark. I call him good old man, although many are of the opinion that he was not good, because he suffered his sons to be wicked; and indeed his fault was great. But surely he was a good man, and I have two reasons to prove it. First, in that he took the punishment of his iniquity so patiently: "It is the Lord: let Him do what seemeth Him good." And secondly, he was a good man, as his care for the ark shows: "He sat trembling for the ark."

Now the ark was a type of three things:

First, it was a type of Jesus Christ; for as God

spoke from the ark, so God speaks to us by Christ.

Secondly, it was a type of the ordinances of Christ; for as God communicated Himself by the ark, so God by His ordinances communicates His counsels, comforts, and grace to his people. So, I have showed you what the ark was.

I shall gather two observations from the words of the text:

I. When the ark of God is in danger of being lost, the people of God have thoughtful heads and trembling hearts.

II. A true child of God is more troubled, and more anxious what shall become of the ark, than what shall become of wife and children or estate.

I shall begin with the first doctrine, namely, that when the ark of God is in danger of being lost, the people of God have thoughtful heads and trembling hearts. Or, if I may put this doctrine in a gospel dress, take it this way: *when the gospel is in danger of being lost, when gospel-ordinances and gospel-ministers are in danger of being lost, then the people of God have trembling heads, and concerned and anxious hearts about it.*

Mark what I say. I do not say *when the ark is lost,* for that was death to old Eli, that broke his neck, and it cost the life of Eli's daughter-in-law. When the ark of God was taken, she took no comfort in her child; though a man child, she regarded it not. For, "the glory is departed from Israel, the ark of God is taken."

I do not say when the ark of God is lost; but I say when it is in *danger* of being lost. When the gospel is in danger, the ministers of the gospel in danger, and the ordinances in danger of being lost, then the people of God have thoughtful heads and anxious hearts. When God threatened the Israelites that He would not go with them, they were troubled for the loss of God's presence, and would not put on their ornaments. "I will not go up in the midst of thee, for thou art a stiff-necked people, lest I consume thee in the way. And when the people heard these evil tidings, they mourned, and no man did put on him his ornaments," Exodus 33:3-4. "And it came to pass while the ark abode in Kirjath-jearim, that the time was long, for it was twenty years, and all the house of Israel lamented after the Lord," 1 Samuel 7:2, that is after the presence of God, speaking from the ark. In 2 Samuel 11:10-11 David would have had Uriah to go down to his house and make merry; but Uriah said to David, "The ark, and Israel, and Judah abide in tents; and my lord Joab, and the servants of my Lord, are encamped in the open fields: shall I then go into mine house to eat and to drink, and to lie with my wife? As thou livest, and as thy soul liveth, I will not do this thing." In 1 Kings 19:10 Elijah says, "I have been very jealous for the Lord God of hosts, for the children of Israel have forsaken thy covenant, thrown down thine altars, and slain thy prophets with the sword, and I, even I only, am left, and they seek my life to take it away." So, you see when the ark is in danger, the people of God mourn and are sorrowful.

There are four reasons why the people of God are so much troubled when the ark of God is in danger.

1. Because of the great love they bear to the ark of God. As "the Lord loveth the gates of Sion, more than all the dwellings of Jacob," (Psalm 87:2), so the people of God love the ordinances of God, and the faithful ministers of Christ. "Lord I have loved the habitation of Thy house, and the place where Thine honor dwelleth," (Psalm 26:8). "One thing have I desired of the Lord all the days of my life, to behold the beauty of the Lord, and to enquire in His temple," (Psalm 27:4). Now love stirs up the affections, as young Croesus who, though he was dumb, yet seeing his father likely to be killed, cried out," Do not kill my father." Such is the love of the saints of

God to the ark, that they cannot be silent until the Lord make "the righteousness thereof go forth as brightness, and the salvation thereof as a lamp that burneth," (Isaiah 62:1).

2. The people of God are troubled when the ark is in danger because of the personal interest they have in the ark of God.

3. The people of God are much troubled when the ark is in danger, because of the mischiefs that come upon a nation when the ark of God is lost. Woe to that nation when the ark is gone! The heathen Greeks had the image of Apollo, and they conceived that as long as that image was preserved among them they could never be worsted, but must be preserved. The Romans had a buckler, concerning which they had a tradition, that as long as that buckler was preserved, Rome could not be taken. I will give a hint of what happens when the ark of God is lost.

When the ark of God is taken, "the ways of Zion mourn, and none come to the solemn feasts," (Lamentations 1:4). This was the complaint of the church and matter of sadness.

When the ark of God is taken, the ministers of Christ are driven into corners. This is matter of heart-trembling.

When the ark of God is taken, the souls of many are in danger. When the gospel is gone, your souls are in hazard. There is cause of sadness.

When the ark of God is taken, the enemies of God blaspheme, and are ready to say, "Where is your God?" Then do the enemies of God triumph. "As with a sword in my bones mine enemies reproach me: while they say daily unto me, Where is thy God?" (Psalm 42:10).

When the ark of God is taken, Jesus Christ is trampled underfoot, and the ordinances of God defiled and trampled on; and then blasphemy and atheism come in like an armed man.

4. The people of God must needs tremble when the ark is in danger, because they share the responsibility for losing of the ark. It was this which made old Eli so much troubled, because he knew it was for his sin that God suffered the ark to be taken. He knew that his own guilt in not punishing his two sons, was one cause of that great slaughter the people of Israel met with; and that made him tremble. There is no person here in this congregation, but his heart will tell him that he has contributed something towards the loss of the ark. None of us is so holy but our consciences must accuse us. We have done something that might cause God to take the ark from us, and therefore Mr. Bradford, that blessed martyr, said in his prayer, "Lord it was my unthankfulness for the gospel, that brought in popery in Queen Mary's days; and my unfruitfulness under the gospel that was the cause of the untimely death of King Edward the Sixth." Again, those that fled in Queen Mary's days sadly complained that they were the cause of God's taking away the gospel from England. O beloved, it is for your sin and my sin that the ark of God is in danger; and therefore the Lord gives us trembling and burdened hearts as to what shall become of the ark.

I come now to the *application*.

Use 1. If it is the mark of a true child of God to be concerned when the ark of God is in danger, and to have such a trembling heart for fear of the ark, then this is a certain sign there are but few that are the children of God in truth. O where is the man, and where is the woman, that like old Eli sits watching and trembling for fear of the ark? And the reasons for watching and trembling are these:

First, *the many sins in this nation.* For let me tell you, there is not one sin for which God ever took away the ark from any people, but it is to be found in England. Did the church of Ephesus lose the candlestick, because they had lost their first love? And have not we lost our first love to the gospel and to the ordinances? And did the church of Laodicea lose the candlestick, because of luke-warmness? And are not we lukewarm? Did the people of Israel, as here in the text, lose the ark, because they abhorred the offerings of God? And do you not so? Are not the sins of Israel amongst us? And the sins of Germany, and the sins of all other nations, about us. And is there any man here before God this day, in this congregation, who can consider the great unthankfulness of this nation, and the great profaneness and wickedness of this nation, and not conclude that the ark is in danger, and that God may justly take the ark from us?

I might tell you of the drunkenness, adultery, covetousness, injustice, uncharitableness, and such like sins that abound among us. I might tell you of sanctuary sins, profanation of Sabbath and sacraments, our unthankfulness, and unfruitfulness, and unworthy walking under the gospel. And you of this place, God may very well take the ark from you; and indeed it was out of the great interest I had in you (the which while I live, I shall never own), and from that great affection and respect I had to you, that I would not send you home this day without a sermon, and let you go without a blessing. Now can any of you in this parish, and this congregation, can any of you say, *God may not justly take the gospel from you?*

The second reason for trembling is *the discontents and divisions of the nation.* As Christ says, "A nation divided against itself cannot stand;" but I leave these things to your consideration. I believe there is none here but will confess the ark of God is in danger of being lost. But now where are our Elis to sit watching and trembling for fear of the ark? Where is the wife of Phinehas who would not be comforted, because the ark of God was taken? Where are our Moses, our Elijahs, our Uriahs? Where are they that lay to heart the dangers of the ark? You complain of taxes, decay of trading, of this civil burden, and that civil burden, but where is the man or woman that complains of this misery, the loss of the ark? Most of you are like Gallio; "he cared for none of these things;" if it had been a civil matter, then he would have meddled with it; but for religion, he cared not for that. Every man is troubled about "his own" and "your own," and about civil matters; but who lays to heart, and who regards what shall become of *religion?* There is a strange kind of indifference and luke-warmness on most people's spirits. So long as their trading goes on, and their civil burdens are removed, they do not care what becomes of the ark. There is a text of Scripture—I shall not spend much time in opening it, but I would have you well consider it—Hosea 7:9, "Strangers have devoured his strength and he knoweth it not; yea grey hairs are here and there upon him, yet he knoweth not." Shall I say grey hairs are upon the gospel? I do not come here to prophesy; I do not say the gospel is *dying,* but I do say it has *grey hairs,* for you have had the gospel a hundred years and above, and therefore it is in its old age. And I dare challenge any scholar to show me an example of a nation that has enjoyed the gospel for a hundred years together. Now that grey hairs belong to a hundred years is no wonder. Well grey hairs are here and there, and yet no man lays it to heart.

Now I shall show you what a great sin it is not to be affected with the danger that the ark of God is in. Consider but three particulars:

First, it is a sign *you do not love the gospel.* If you

had any love to it, you would be troubled more for the danger of the ark, than for any outward danger whatsoever.

Secondly, it is a sign *you have no interest in the gospel*, for interest would stir up your affections. It is a sign you are not concerned in the gospel, for if you were concerned it, you would be affected with it, as even it was with those that were interested in those persons that were in the lamentable fire last week; it was impossible that they should be unaffected. And so it is a sign you have no interest in God and Christ, if your hearts do not tremble for fear the ark be lost.

Thirdly, *there is a curse of God* pronounced against all those that do not lay to heart the affliction of Joseph. "Woe be to them that are at ease in Sion, and trust in the mountains of Samaria...ye that put far away the evil day...that lie upon beds of ivory, and stretch themselves upon their couches: that eat the lambs out of the flock, and the calves out of the midst of the stall: that chant to the sound of the viol, and invent to themselves instruments of music...that drink wine in bowls, and anoint themselves with the chief ointments: but they are not grieved for the affliction of Joseph," Amos 6:1-6. Woe be to you that enjoy your fullness of outward things, and make merry therewith, and never consider the afflictions of God's people, and the danger of the ark.

Use 2. Let me, by way of exhortation, beseech you all whom God by a providence has so unexpectedly brought together this day to hear me (and there may be a good providence in it). I say, let me beseech you all to declare you are the people of God in deed and in truth, by following the example of old Eli, to be very concerned for the ark of God, and let me exhort you to five particulars:

First, let me persuade you to believe that the gospel is not entailed on England; England has no

Letters Patent of the gospel; the gospel is removable. God took away the ark, but the temple also. He unchurched the Jews, he unchurched the seven churches of Asia, and we do not know how soon He may unchurch us. I know no warrant we have to think that we shall have the gospel another hundred years. God knows how to remove his candlestick, but not to destroy it. God often removes the church, but does not destroy it. God removed His church out of the East; the Greek churches were famous churches, but God removed them, and now the Turk overspreads that country.

Secondly, I would persuade you that England's ark is in *danger of being lost*, even were it only for the sins of England, those prodigious iniquities amongst us, and that strange unheard of ingratitude that is in the land. But I will say no more of that, because I would speak nothing but what becomes a sober minister of the gospel.

Thirdly, I would persuade you, and O that I could raise you up to old Eli's practice, "He sat watching; for his heart trembled of the ark." He had a thoughtful head and an aching heart for the ark of God that was in great danger. That I might move you to this, *consider what a sad condition we are in*, if the ark is taken. What good will your estate do you? Or what good will your business do you if the gospel be gone? Where does England excel other places? There is more wealth in Turkey than in England, and the other heathen nations have more of the glory of the world than any Christian king has. Where is the glory of England? Is it not Christianity? Where is the glory of Christianity but the gospel? If the gospel is gone, our glory is gone. Pray, remember Eli's daughter-in-law, the wife of Phinehas. She did not hearken, though a man child was born, and would receive no comfort, but called his name Ichabod, for "the glory is departed from Israel; the ark of God is taken." O, when the glory is gone, who would desire to live? I am loth to tell you the story of Chrysostom; he was but one man, yet when he was banished from Constantinople, the people all petitioned for him, and said that they could as well lose the sun out of the firmament as lose Chrysostom from among them.

Fourthly, let me persuade you *not to mourn immoderately*, neither be discouraged. I would willingly speak something to comfort you before I leave you. I do not know by what strange providence I came here this day, and the Lord knows when I shall speak to you again: therefore I would not send you home comfortless. O therefore mourn not as without hope, for I have four arguments to persuade me that the ark of God will not be lost, though it is in danger.

(1.) Because God has done great things already for this nation. I argue like Manoah's wife, *Surely, if God had intended to destroy us, He would not have done what He has done for us.* He who has done so much for us will not now forsake us. And therefore though our hearts tremble, yet let them not sink within us.

(2.) I argue from the abundance of praying people that are in this nation. There are many that night and day pray unto God that the ark may not be taken; and let me assure you, God will never forsake a praying and a reforming people. When God intends to destroy a nation, and take away the ark, He takes away the spirit of prayer; but where God gives the spirit of prayer, there God will continue the ark. You all know, that if there had been but ten good men in those five cities, God would have spared them. We have many hundreds that fear God in this nation, that do not give God rest, but night and day pray to God for this land. And who knows but for their sakes God will spare the ark?

(3.) Another ground of comfort is that God has here dealt with England, not by way of rule, but by way of prerogative. We have had sins fitted to unchurch us all the reign of Queen Elizabeth, and King James, and the godly ministers have been threatened with ruin from year to year; but God has here saved England by prerogative. God has spared us because he will spare us, according to that text, "I will be gracious to whom I will be gracious." God will not be tied to His own rule, and who knows but God will deliver us again?

(4.) Another ground of comfort is that God is now pouring out His vials upon Antichrist, and all this shall end in the ruin of Antichrist. God is pouring forth his vials upon the throne of the beast, and all these transactions shall end in the ruin of Antichrist. Though some drops of these vials may light upon the Reformed churches, and they may smart for a while, and God may severely punish them, yet it will be but for a little while. God may scourge all the Reformed churches before these vials are fully poured out, and persecution may go through them all; the which I call drops of these vials, but the vials are intended for Antichrist. And whatever becomes of us, yet our children, and our children's children, shall see the outcome of the vials poured out upon the whore of Babylon. This I speak for your comfort.

Fifthly, I am to exhort you that you would all of you *contribute your utmost endeavor to keep the ark of God from being taken.* And here I shall show you what magistrates, ministers and the people should do.

I shall say but little about what magistrates should do, because I am not now to speak to them. They are to use their authority for the settling of the ark; for the ark of the covenant will be like the ark of Noah always floating upon the waters, until the magistrates settle it. Thus it was with David, 2 Samuel 6:1-2, who gathered together all the chosen men of Israel, and the heads of the tribes, the nobles, and the chief of the fathers of the children of Israel at Jerusalem with a great deal of pomp, to bring up the ark of the covenant of the Lord into its place. O that God would encourage our nobles and magistrates that they might be concerned to settle the ark. Magistrates must not be as the Philistines; they had the ark, but what did they do with it? They set it up in the house of Dagon, but Dagon and the ark could never agree. Where false religion comes in at one door, true religion goes out at the other. You must not put the ark and Dagon together.

What must the ministers do to keep the ark from being lost? They must endeavor after holiness. The ark will never stand steady, nor prosper upon the shoulders of Hophni and Phinehas. A wicked, profane, drunken ministry will never settle the ark. It must be the sober, pious, godly ministers that must do it. How holy must they be that draw nigh to the God of holiness!

What must the people of God do, that the ark may not be lost? There are five things I shall commend unto you, and then commend you to God.

(1.) *You must not idolize the ark.* That was the sin of the people in the text. They thought the very presence of the ark would excuse them, and keep them safe, and therefore, they carried the ark into the camp. Though they did not reform, and did not repent, yet they thought the ark would save them. So there are many that think the ark will save them, though they are never so wicked. But nothing will secure a nation, but repentance and reformation.

(2.) *Do not undervalue the ark.* This was Michal's sin, 2 Samuel 6:14-23. When David danced before the ark, Michal mocked him, and despised him in her heart, "but," said he "it was before the Lord, and if this be vile, I will yet be more vile." Some men begin to say, what need have we of preaching? Will not reading prayers serve? Others say, what do we need of so much preaching? Will not once a day serve? Now this is to undervalue the ark. Therefore let us say as David: *If to preach the word, and to fast and pray for the nation is vile, then I will yet be more vile.*

(3.) *We must not pry into the ark.* This was the sin of the men of Bethshemesh. "They looked into the ark, and God smote them, and cut off fifty thousand and threescore and ten men," (1 Samuel 6:19). Be not too curious in searching where God has not discovered or revealed. For example, there are great thoughts of heart as to when God will deliver His people, and set His churches at liberty; and many men talk much of the year 1666. Some say that shall be the year in which Antichrist shall be destroyed. And there are some strange impressions upon the hearts of many learned men as to that year. Some go to the year 1669, and others pitch upon other times. But, truly, if you will have my judgment, and I am glad of this opportunity to tell you, this is to pry too much into the ark. Remember the text, "It is not for you to know the times or the seasons which the Father hath put in His own power," (Acts 1:7). And so to fasten upon any particular time, if you find you are deceived, this is the way to make you atheists, and thus afterwards you will believe nothing. Those ministers do no service, or rather ill service, to the church of God, that fix upon the times and seasons.

A Popish author says that in the year 1000 there was a general belief over the Christian world, that the day of judgment should be that year; but when they saw it did not happen, they fell to their old sinning again, and were worse than before, and believed nothing. Well God's time is the best, therefore let us not pry too much into the ark.

(4.) *You must not meddle with the ark*, unless you have a lawful call to meddle with it. This was the sin of Uzzah, 2 Samuel 6:6-7. The ark was in danger of falling, and he, good man, meaning no hurt, to support the ark took hold of it; but for so doing, he destroyed himself, and made a breach, and hindered the carrying home of the ark at that time.

We have had a great deal of disorder heretofore; and an abundance of well-minded people have usurped the ministerial office. They were afraid the ark was falling, and therefore they touched the ark, they laid hold on the ark; but their touching the ark had undone the ark, and themselves too. O take heed of touching the ark.

(5.) If ever you would preserve the ark, then keep the covenant of the ark; keep the law which the ark preserves. The ark was a place in which the two tables of Law were kept. Keep the law, and God will keep the ark. But if you break the law, you will forfeit the ark. The ark was called the ark of the *covenant.* Keep covenant with God, and God will preserve the ark. But if you break the covenant of the ark, the covenant made in baptism, that covenant often renewed in the sacrament, if you break covenant, God will take away the ark.

Now interest stirs up affection, just as when a man is concerned when a friend's house is on fire. You had a lamentable and sad providence this last week, and it is not to be forgotten — how suddenly in all our feastings, God may dash all our mirth. Now consider how affected they were that had an interest in the ark. God is the haven of the children of God, the portion and inheritance of the children of God; and when God begins to forsake them, they cannot but be afflicted and troubled. The ordinances of God are the jewels of a Christian, and the treasure of a Christian: and the loss of them cannot but trouble him. And Jesus Christ is the joy of a Christian, and therefore when Christ is departing, he cannot but be much afflicted by it.

FINIS

Other Books Published by Puritan Publications

The Covenant of Works and the Covenant of Grace – by Edmund Calamy (1600-1666)

The Christian's Combat Against the Devil - Christopher Love (1618-1651)

The Believer's Privileges in the Covenant of Grace - Thomas Watson (1620-1686)

The Lord's Voice Cries to the City: A Biblical Guide for Hearing the Word of God Preached - by C. Matthew McMahon

Christ Inviting Sinners to Come to Him for Rest - by Jeremiah Burroughs (1599-1646)

The Duty of Reformation in Light of God's Mercies - by Thomas Gouge (1605-1681)

A Comfort for the Afflicted Christian - by William Plumer (1802-1880)

A Glimpse of God's Glory - Thomas Hodges (1600-1672)

God's Just Desertion of the Unjust, and Other Works - by Hannibal Gammon (1585-1674)

The Christian's Union, Communion and Conformity to Jesus Christ In His Death and Resurrection - by John Brinsley (1600-1665)